THE WEALTH OF CHOICES

ALSO BY ALAN MURRAY

Showdown at Gucci Gulch

(with Jeffrey H. Birnbaum)

The Wealth of Choices

How the New Economy Puts Power in Your Hands and Money in Your Pocket

ALAN MURRAY

CROWN
BUSINESS
NEW YORK

Published by Crown Publishers, New York, New York. Member of
the Crown Publishing Group.

Random House, Inc., New York, Toronto, London, Sydney, Auckland
www.randomhouse.com

CROWN Business is a trademark of Random House, Inc.

Design by Robert C. Olsson

Library of Congress Cataloging-in-Publication Data
Murray, Alan S., 1954-
The wealth of choices : how the new economy puts power in your hands and
money in your pocket / Alan Murray.
       p.   cm.
Includes index.
1. United States—Economic conditions—1981–   2. United States—Economic
     policy—1993–   3. Competition, International.   I. Title.
       HC106.82.M87   2000
338.973—dc21   99-057773
ISBN 0-8129-3266-8

10   9   8   7   6   5   4   3   2   1

First Edition

To my father, who taught me the value of money,
To my mother, who taught me the value of everything else,
To my wife, Lori, who gave me life's most valuable treasures,
Especially, Lucyann and Amanda

CONTENTS

Contents

THE WEALTH OF CHOICES

1

Not My Father's Economy

My first foray into national journalism came in 1976, when *Life* magazine invited me to write a brief essay for a special edition about youth in America. Then a junior at the University of North Carolina, and still very much an adolescent, I took the opportunity to complain about my father:

> When I first came to the university, my father sent me packets of articles from *The Wall Street Journal* and *Fortune* magazine that praised the virtues of free enterprise. Someone had told him that all college professors had socialist tendencies, and that many were outright Marxists, Maoists, or both.

I thought of that article in October of 1998, while flying home to Chattanooga, Tennessee, to attend my father's funeral. His fear for me in those days had been that I was part of a lost generation. We had missed the character-building hardships of the Great Depression, and as a result, we would never fully appreciate the value of the dollar and never understand the power of the market economy—

or, as the title of one free-market tribute he sent me called it, *The Incredible Bread-Making Machine*. The nation and the world, he worried, were headed toward some sort of inevitable socialist decline. And the way would be led by his son, who preferred poetry to physics.

How surprised he must have been at the way things turned out. During the last year of his life, confined to his bed with cancer, he took comfort in tuning the television to CNBC and seeing me, with stock market quotes streaming across my chest, the Dow Jones average planted firmly on my shoulder, and the words *The Wall Street Journal* nestled just below my chin.

But he must have been even more surprised to see how the world changed in that last quarter-century of his life. There was no socialist decline, no creeping expansion of the welfare state. Instead, just the opposite happened. The incredible bread-making machine proved more pervasive, more powerful, more incredible than he or anyone else could have imagined back in 1976.

The triumph of capitalism is, by now, a well-known story. British prime minister Margaret Thatcher and President Ronald Reagan heralded in a revitalization of the market economies of the West, while Soviet prime ministers Mikhail Gorbachev and Boris Yeltsin signaled the end of communism. The dramatic collapse of the Berlin Wall allowed the triumphant doctrine to spill over into every corner of the globe, with only a handful of people out of its powerful reach. The global financial crisis of the late 1990s underscored the darker side of markets and prompted some ponderous reevaluations of the free-market faith, but produced no substitutes. Today, the entire world agrees with my father: capitalism, whatever its faults, beats the alternatives.

Less widely appreciated, however, is just how profoundly the American economy has changed in those same two decades. No barbed-wire-laced concrete walls needed to fall here, and no arrogant tyrants needed toppling. No hidebound central-planning bureaucracies were dismantled. Yet the changes here, while less heralded, were no less revolutionary; perhaps even more so.

Consider what life was like just one generation ago. Sure, if you wanted to buy breakfast cereal, the market gave you options. But in other ways, markets were limited, and choices restrained. On Lookout Mountain, where I grew up, our electricity was provided by one company, the Electric Power Board, and our phone service, like every other American's, came courtesy of Ma Bell. When we were sick, we went to the family doctor and we bought medicine from the neighborhood druggist. And if we were very sick, we went to the local hospital—no choices necessary. Television options were limited to UHF and VHF; banks were open from nine to three.

Airline fares were fixed at levels far higher than even affluent folks like us could easily afford. So when we traveled, we took the car—a station wagon purchased at Andy Trotter's Pontiac. When the car broke down, which it often did, my father turned red in the face and let loose a string of curses that would end with a threat to "take this car and drive it right into Andy Trotter's swimming pool." It never occurred to me to ask why he kept buying cars from the cursed Mr. Trotter. The answer was obvious: Mr. Trotter was the only Pontiac dealer in town, and General Motors made the only affordable station wagon.

It was a simpler time. Fewer choices meant less complexity, less confusion. Businesses were more likely to treat their workers like family. Wages weren't allowed to diverge too much, for fear of creating rivalry in the company. Employment was often for life. Things were stable, comfortable, and predictable.

But that world was a far cry from the picture of a competitive economy portrayed in *The Incredible Bread-Making Machine,* or in any economic textbook. And it was a far, far, far cry from where we are today.

Today, the basic market principles of competition and choice have swept into every aspect of American life. Consumers face a bewildering array of choices not just for cereal, but for air travel, phone service, medical care, even postal service. In parts of the country, home owners have begun choosing from a menu of companies for their electricity. Health care has undergone a radical market-driven transformation, and education is following not too far behind. If you want to buy a car today, you start by going on the Internet and shopping for the best price available at any dealership within a thousand miles. The same goes for countless other consumer products.

Companies that seemed like unshakable behemoths a generation ago now fight like scrappy entrepreneurs against foreign firms and ever-emerging domestic competitors. Vast fortunes are made, literally overnight. Workers have become free agents, shifting jobs frequently and feeling little loyalty to their employers, who show little loyalty in return.

The world has gotten smaller; competition has gotten more intense; choices have become more plentiful.

Not long ago, former Senator Nancy Kassebaum asked me to give a dinner speech to the U.S.–Turkey Business Council, which she co-chairs. I immediately agreed. Senator Kassebaum had employed my wife, Lori, for nearly a decade and is a wonderful, public-spirited politician. I would do almost anything she asked.

But after arriving at the dinner, I began to regret my decision. It was a raucous group of more than six hundred people who talked right through the master of ceremonies' opening jokes. My dinner partner, the wife of the U.S. ambassador to Turkey, leaned over and whispered: "Don't worry. This is what *all* Turkish dinners are like."

The crowd turned appreciatively silent, however, when I got to the thesis of my short talk: The New Economy, I told them, is like the Istanbul bazaar, that five-hundred-year-old covered maze where thousands of vendors sell carpets and curios, icons and samovars. The orderly world of a generation ago, with its limited choices and fixed prices and clear lines of distribution, is being transformed into a chaotic, bustling, teeming global marketplace. Countless sellers court countless buyers, with an endless array of merchandise. Prices aren't fixed. Each merchant tries to extract the highest price for his wares; but each customer has the power to walk to the next booth in search of a better deal.

The metaphor was right for the crowd, but it is also right for the times. The New Economy is, in a strange way, a return to something older—a world where the economy's rhythm is determined by countless transactions among individual buyers and sellers, rather than being a staid dance among corporate hierarchies. Globalization, deregulation, and digitization are turning the entire world into a modern version of the Istanbul bazaar.

But there is a new twist: pervasive information. Throughout capitalism's history, sellers have usually had an edge over buyers, because they have been better informed. The merchant in the bazaar knew more than the buyer about the quality of the carpet he was hawking and knew what it cost him to acquire.

Today, the tables have been turned. With a little effort, the consumer has access to information about the quality and cost of almost any product or service he or she chooses to buy. As the new millennium begins, the power balance, for the first time in the history of capitalism, has shifted in the consumer's favor. Consumers come to the bazaar armed not only with choices, but with knowledge, and the result of that combination is power.

Consider the case of Norman Ornstein, a political scientist and one of Washington's most peripatetic television commentators. Recently, he decided he wanted to buy a Lexus sport utility vehicle. (Talking-head-dom has been a lucrative occupation for Norm.) Instead of driving to the nearest dealer, he logged on to the Internet, visited the manufacturer's website, read reviews of the car in *Road and Track,* and then logged on to Auto-by-Tel (Autobytel.com). He entered the exact specifications of the car he wanted to buy.

The next day, Norm got a call from a Lexus dealership in Alexandria, Virginia, offering him a good price on the car he wanted. It was $1,200 below list—for a car that was in short supply and that almost everyone else was selling at full list price. Shortly thereafter, his wife, Judy, went to a nearby Lexus dealer in Rockville, Maryland, test-drove the car, and then offered to pay that dealer the same price suggested by Auto-by-Tel, and not a penny more. The dealer agreed.

Norm had a similar experience when he needed to buy a new tennis racket to help ease the pain of tennis elbow. First, he visited a tennis store just a block away from his office and tried out several different rackets, even taking some home for the weekend to play with them. He found the titanium racket he wanted, but it was expensive—nearly $350. By visiting an Internet site called playpro.com, he found a dealer who was willing to ship him the same racket for a price just above $200.

Norm returned to the tennis shop and cut a deal. "I'm willing to pay a premium for your help and service," he said. "But I'm not a fool." They settled on a price of $250. The store's owner, Darrell Haines, says this was not the first or last time someone had come in asking him to match an Internet price. Indeed, he said, it happens about once a week.

In the New Economy, these sorts of stories are becoming commonplace. The old economy's watchword was *caveat emptor,* "Let the buyer beware." But today, it's the seller who must beware, because the buyer may be arriving armed with information.

I recently asked a prominent doctor to tell me the biggest change that has occurred in his business in the last decade. I expected to hear a rant against managed care. But he said the biggest change in his business is this: patients come to him with information. They research their illnesses before they arrive at his office. They have opinions about the options for their treatment. And they expect *him* to discuss all this openly with them. That's not the way it was a generation ago.

The economics-textbook notion of perfect competition, with countless buyers facing countless sellers, all armed with the same information, all aggressively pursuing their own interests, is closer to reality today than it has ever been before. The world, in short, has become a more perfect bazaar.

New Economy, New Rules

What does all this mean for you? Quite a lot. This isn't your father's economy, so your father's rules for managing financial affairs won't work any longer. New rules are needed.

This book is intended to do two things: First, provide a simple explanation of what the New Economy is and how it came about and, second, provide some simple but valuable rules for coping with and conquering that economy. In the process, it will clear your mind of antiques and cobwebs, in order to make room for new furnishings.

Can the rules of financial management really be so different today? You bet. For starters, here's a sampling of some of yesterday's financial wisdom and the new rules that need to replace it.

Your father told you: Don't use credit cards, and don't buy annuities or other investment products from an insurance company

That's the kind of uncompromising advice you'll find in almost every personal finance book on the market. And it used to be good advice. But no longer.

There was a time when all credit cards charged usuriously high interest rates and all annuities included high fees and low returns. But in the New Economy, the powers of competition are so uncompromising and intense that everyone—even credit card companies and insurance companies—must bend to them. Companies will still try to fleece the unsuspecting consumer. But if you pay attention, you can get good value for your money.

Take credit cards. I have an annual spring bulge in my expenses, thanks to tax bills, tuition bills, and a few other unpleasant expenses that all seem to crop up at the same time. I use credit cards to manage that bulge.

Every couple of weeks, I get another letter in the mail asking me to sign up for a new credit card that offers a 3.9 or 4.9 or 5.9 percent "introductory rate," usually lasting six to nine months. Each offer comes with an easy-to-use form that lets me transfer balances from an old card. So in the spring, I let my balances build up and I switch cards when necessary to keep the rate down. It's easy, and it's cheap.

Now, no one is going to get rich rolling over credit card balances. But there is a lesson here. Credit card companies that used to routinely charge 18 percent interest have decided to meet the stiff competition of the New Economy by offering teaser rates. Their hope is that once you switch, you won't switch again. But if you understand the new competition, you'll become a frequent switcher. Move your balances every six months, and you'll end up ahead.

The story on annuities is much the same. These are hybrid investments that are part insurance, part mutual fund. Until recently, they were invariably a rip-off, charging high, often hidden, fees and then using the proceeds to pay large commissions to brokers, who in turn eagerly pushed the products on their unsuspecting customers. Not surprisingly, annuities got a bad name.

But competition and information have transformed this business, like so many others. Mutual fund companies such as Vanguard and T. Rowe Price now offer variable annuities with low fees and attractive investment options. They still don't make sense for everyone. But armed with the right information—available on websites like insure.com and annuity.com—the consumer can get a good buy.

The world is still full of people eager to make you buy things you don't need at prices higher than you should pay. But if you keep your head up and spend the small amount of time necessary to arm yourself with information, you can demand better—and most likely you'll get it.

In the New Economy, competition forces companies to respond to the demands of informed consumers—or go out of business.

Your father said: Your home is your nest egg; the bigger the mortgage, the better

For a generation of Americans, that was probably the best financial advice anyone could give. But not today. And most financial guides haven't caught up with the new reality.

If you bought a house in the early 1970s, odds are that by the late '80s you had made a bundle. Home owners found the accumulated equity in their house could help finance college or pay for retirement. In a time of inflation, it was the ultimate hedge.

My wife and I enjoyed only a part of that boom. The Sears house we bought on the outskirts of Georgetown in 1983 for $130,000 sold for $300,000 only five years later.

Others, who started earlier, scored even more spectacular gains. Ken Bacon, who was my first editor at *The Wall Street Journal,* went on to become the chief spokesman at the Pentagon. Through a bit of bad luck, he gained fame as the employer of Monica Lewinsky and Linda Tripp; later, he was the steady voice of the war in Kosovo. But in real estate, he couldn't have been luckier.

He and his wife bought their first house in 1969, in the shadow of the Capitol building, for $36,000. They put another $14,000 into it and sold it in 1975, getting back almost double their money. That year, they bought their next house, just past Georgetown University, for $125,000. Today it's worth at least five times that.

With such spectacular gains, Americans came to think of their homes as their very best investment; and a bigger home, or even two homes, only made them feel financially wiser.

But here's the catch: That investment miracle was driven by inflation. Houses were a safe harbor against the ravages of price increases. Mortgages shrank in relation to inflation-driven incomes. And Uncle Sam made the deal sweeter by providing a generous tax break for inflation-swollen interest payments.

Those days are gone. Inflation appears to have been tamed, thanks to the efforts of Paul Volcker, Alan Greenspan, and a generation of tough-minded central bankers around the globe. And the dynamics of the New Economy will help to keep it from coming back. In the old days, unemployment of 4 or 5 percent would have led to inflation, as companies felt forced to pay more to workers and then raise prices accordingly. Today, fierce competition seems to have helped keep a lid on prices. Certain cities and neighborhoods have hot housing markets, but overall, houses have become, well, a place to live. As investments, they are no longer the best alternative. And mortgages are no longer the bargain they once were, in spite of relatively low rates.

Many financial advisers are still peddling the wisdom learned yesterday. "We must buy today to avoid tomorrow's price increase," writes Ric Edelman in the introduction to his best-selling guide *The Truth About Money*. And on mortgages, he advises that you should "carry a *huge* one—and *never* pay it off."

Good advice a decade ago. Not so today. Consider this: If you suddenly found $100,000, what would you do with it? Invest, or pay off your mortgage? If you pay 7 percent on your mortgage and are in the 25 percent tax bracket, the true cost of that mortgage is 5.25 percent. If you can invest tax-free in an IRA or 401(k) plan, *perhaps* you can get a better rate of return than 5.25 percent and come out ahead. If your investments are taxable, however, the odds start to move against you. You may end up earning less than the 5.25 percent you are paying out in mortgage interest. Ignoring Ric Edelman and using the money to pay off your mortgage could make perfect sense.

Old habits die hard, and inflation created a lot of habits. Today, senior citizens bellyache when their social security cost-of-living increase comes in at less than 2 percent. Factory workers gripe about annual pay increases of only 3 percent. Savers complain that their money market account brings in only 3 or 4 percent, when it used to earn 5 or 6 percent. No one is quite willing to accept that inflation was merely a mirage, and now it's gone.

In the New Economy, inflation has been suppressed. Get over it.

Your father said: Location, location, location

Wake up and smell the silicon. In the old economy, geography meant everything. "Convenience" referred to location; the store nearest your house was most likely to get your business. In the new economy, distance has been conquered. "Convenience" is Amazon.com.

The Internet has been the most powerful culprit in the death of distance. But it only accelerated a trend that was already well under way.

Federal Reserve Board chairman Alan Greenspan likes to point out that the physical weight of the nation's output of goods and services changed little in the latter half of the twentieth century, while its value increased more than twenty-fold. In other words, things are getting smaller and lighter. Plastic has replaced steel; transistors have replaced vacuum tubes; fiber optic cable has replaced tons of copper wire. Most important, software has become more valuable than hardware. Knowledge has become the number one source of value in the New Economy, and knowledge weighs very little indeed.

As the physical substance of the nation's output vanishes, physical geography becomes less important. Products can move on airplanes instead of ships or can be bounced off satellites instead of being shipped on airplanes.

Remember the Club of Rome? They were the wise men and women who, in the 1970s, issued dire warnings about the need to keep the world from running out of physical resources. They needed an upgrade. The last generation ignored their warnings, and the world survived. Much of today's consumption—from video games to Viagra pills—draws little from the earth's physical resources. (In the meantime, the Club of Rome has acquired a website—clubofrome.com.)

New Economy rule: The world has become smaller, and all within your reach.

In your father's economy, prices were fixed; everyone paid the same amount

When I was growing up, it never occurred to me to walk into Sam Robinson's drugstore and demand a 20 percent discount. The price was marked, and everyone paid it. Or at least, so I thought.

But in the New Economy, prices have gone squishy. If you pay full price, you're a chump.

Airlines are the most obvious example. If you want to start a riot, get all the passengers on an airplane to confess what they paid for their tickets. The differences are astounding. On a flight from Washington, D.C., to Portland, Oregon, for instance, you're likely to find a business flier, paying the full coach fare of about $2,000 round-trip, sitting next to a tourist who booked a Saturday night stay-over and is paying only $475. Nearby, there could be a traveler who bought a ticket on Priceline.com, which allows you to "name your price," and who paid only $200. And of course, one or two passengers are likely to be flying free with frequent flier miles. All get the same narrow seat, eat the same skimpy snack, and endure the same wait on the runway.

In the New Economy, airline-style price discrimination is rapidly becoming the norm. Take long-distance telephone service. The range of options is mind-numbing. But if you find another long-distance provider who is offering a better deal, call your provider first—odds are, yours will match it.

Washington Post reporter John Schwartz recently wrote of going to a Home Depot store and watching the customer in front of him whip out a coupon for a 10 percent discount. "How do I get a coupon like that?" he asked. After some back-and-forth with the clerk, a manager walked by and said, "Give this man 10 percent off."

Such stories abound. In today's economy, savvy people have learned never to pay the regular rate for a hotel room. Instead they ask, "Don't you have a better rate?" and the bargaining begins.

This, by the way, is one facet of the New Economy that is sharply at odds with the textbook notion of perfect competition. Economics textbooks teach the law of one price for one product. But in the New Economy, price discrimination has become the key to profits. That means consumers have to keep their guard up. Never pay full price; never assume prices are fixed. Choice and information put pricing power in your hands, but it's up to you to exercise that power.

In the New Economy, you can't take any price as a given. Everything is negotiable.

Your father said: Don't squander your money; capital is the key to riches

The old economy was built by men who amassed great quantities of capital. Thrift was the highest virtue. And many prodigal sons and daughters were chastised for "wasting" their inheritance on frivolous travel or endless education. Money was the surest path to wealth.

The New Economy is being built by those who amass great knowledge. A well-trained, supple human mind is the greatest prize, and pursuit of knowledge an increasingly promising road to wealth.

If you doubt that, take a trip to MIT or Stanford University or any other major university and you'll find people who in the last few years have turned their knowledge into enormous wealth. The balance of power has shifted away from those who have capital and toward those who have ideas.

As the value of knowledge rises, of course, so too does the value of education. Consider these simple statistics: In 1970, a college graduate could earn, on average, about $2,667 more annually than a high school graduate. By 1997, that differential had risen to $14,745.

Formal education is one way to accumulate useful knowledge, but not the only way. The history of the New Economy is filled with tales of those who dropped out of college to pursue their interests. The point is this: In the New Economy, the person with the most flexible mind, the broadest array of experience, and the kind of intellectual curiosity and knowledge that define education at its best will continue to be in great demand.

My colleague Walt Mossberg is a wonderful illustration of the change. For years, he rotated through jobs in the Washington bureau of *The Wall Street Journal*, as energy reporter, deputy bureau chief, economics reporter, and defense reporter. But for years, his real passion—which he pursued to the distraction of his family and colleagues alike—was computers. He spent hours tinkering with computer programs, customizing programs for *Journal* reporters, learning about different sorts of software.

Today he has found a new life as one of the nation's leading computer pundits, writing regular columns for *The Wall Street Journal* and *Smart Money* magazine. Computer magnates, eager for a kind word from him, stream in and out of his office. He won't talk about the generous pay package he negotiated with Dow Jones as a result, but it is the envy of the newsroom.

In the New Economy, you need to keep your mind active, open, and engaged, because in the end, it is your best investment.

Your father said: Investing is an insider's game; let someone else do it for you

The investment story of the last two decades has been the explosion of mutual funds in this country. A generation ago, they were unheard of; today, they hold more than $4.5 trillion. We've taken our savings out of the bank and turned them over to professional investors.

But here's a sad fact: In 1998, only 12 percent of mutual fund managers did better than the market averages. In 1999, fund managers did better, but still more than a third were outperformed by the broad market averages.

The truth is, there are no insiders in today's information-besotted economy. Everyone has instant access to the same information. As a result, mutual fund managers struggle to beat the market, even as they charge you fees for the privilege of doing so.

That leaves you with two alternatives. One is to invest your money yourself; with today's technology and information, it's not that hard or time-consuming. The other alternative is to simply invest in an index fund, which is like a mutual fund but has lower fees and simply tracks the movement in an overall market index.

In the New Economy, professional money managers don't know much that you don't.

Your father said: Don't count on social security. It will be bankrupt before you retire

How many times have you heard that warning? It has sunk deep into the consciousness of every American.

But the truth is, social security is one of the surest bets for the future. And the reason is the very same fact that leads some to question the program's solvency: the retirement of the baby boomers.

The baby boom generation is the largest generation in American history. It is heading into retirement at a time when medical science has extended the length of human life. The strain that will be put on our society is daunting. When social security was created, there were 10 working Americans for every 1 retiree. Today there are 3.5. By the middle of the next century, if present trends continue, that number will fall below 2. That means fewer workers paying payroll taxes into the social security trust fund, and more retirees taking money out. The latest projections show the trust fund running out of cash in the year 2034—although the strong economy could stretch that out considerably.

But because it is so large, and because it is so demanding, the baby boom generation is also the most politically potent in American history. As the number of retirees swells, their political clout will swell as well. And make no mistake about it: They will get their social security payments. "I want it *now*" is a refrain that has followed the baby boomers through life; there is no reason to expect it to fade in retirement.

Bottom line: Social security does not, and will not, provide enough money for a lavish retirement. But don't be fooled by the Chicken Littles; it's not going away.

I've talked about what the New Economy is. But it's probably a good idea to mention a few things the New Economy *isn't*.

It isn't an end to recessions. For reasons that are discussed in Chapter 3, the New Economy does seem more resistant to economic downturns than the old one. But ultimately, recessions occur because of human psychology. When the economy has been good for a long time, people are inclined to believe it will get better forever. That leads them to invest more than is justified and spend more than they can afford. Eventually, the bubble bursts, and recession results.

Likewise, the New Economy isn't reason to believe the stock market will move in only one direction. Markets will continue to rise with mass enthusiasm, and fall with mass disappointment. Perhaps the Dow Jones industrial average will soon fulfill the wild predictions of my friend Jim Glassman in the book he co-authored with Kevin Hassett, *Dow 36,000;* but I certainly wouldn't bet much money on it.

In short, while the economy has changed, human nature hasn't.

Finally, there's one recommendation that this book will place before all others: If you aren't on the Internet, get on it now. This is increasingly cheap and increasingly easy. The New Economy is all about information, and the Internet is a revolution in information.

You may never buy a book on Amazon.com or linger in a chat room. But you can use the information that only the Internet can provide to make the most of your future.

To make it even easier on you, I suggest you go straight to wealthofchoices.wsj.com. That's the website for this book, and it will provide you links to the many informational sites mentioned in the following pages.

2

A Quiz

Are You Ready for the New Economy?

The New Economy calls for new ways of thinking about your finances. Answer the following questions; then calculate your score to see if you're prepared. If you score over 150 points, you are off to a good start; score under 50, and you'll need to read this book twice.

1. The last time you bought a car, where did you go first for information?

    A. *Consumer Reports* or a similar consumer magazine

    B. A car broker

    C. The Internet

    D. The local car dealer

2. In the last year, have you:

    A. Switched credit cards to take advantage of introductory rates?

    B. Switched your long-distance phone service to take advantage of a special offer?

    C. Switched both your credit card *and* your long-distance ser-
vice?

    D. Switched neither?

3. *How much of your gross income goes to pay your mortgage?*

    A. More than 40 percent

    B. 30 to 40 percent

    C. 20 to 30 percent

    D. 10 to 20 percent

    E. Less than 10 percent

4. *Lycos is*

    A. A synthetic fabric

    B. An Internet portal

5. *Who is likely to do a better job of finding you cheap airfare?*

    A. Your trusted travel agent

    B. Yourself, using an Internet fare-finder or airline web page

6. *Based on national averages, a college education today is worth how much in additional annual income?*

    A. $500

    B. $5,000

    C. $15,000

7. *Do you get angry that your money market fund only earns 3 or 4 percent interest, when it used to earn 5 or 6 percent?*

    A. Yes

    B. No

8. Mutual funds are a good way to invest because a professional money manager can beat the market and get better returns than you could on your own.

    A. Agree

    B. Disagree

9. In 1992, you got a 6 percent raise. In 1998, you got 4 percent. In which year did you get the better raise?

    A. 1992

    B. 1998

10. For the most part, products are worth more when they are used by fewer people.

    A. True

    B. False

11. When a software product comes in three different versions—standard, professional, and deluxe—which do you buy?

    A. I'm inclined to buy the professional version to be safe, but not extravagant.

    B. I usually buy deluxe because I want the best.

    C. I'll usually buy the standard because it's the cheapest.

12. You walk into a hotel in New York City; the clerk tells you your room will cost $205 a night. Do you:

    A. Accept the rate, because clerks don't have the power to change rates anyway?

    B. Ask if there isn't a better rate available?

13. You're going to have a major operation, and you have to choose between two hospitals. What do you do?

A. Choose a small hospital near your home that seems clean, friendly, and staffed with people you can trust.

B. Choose a large hospital farther away in which doctors perform this operation more often.

C. Investigate both hospitals; then choose the one that has the lowest hospital infection rate.

14. Whether or not a woman gets regular mammograms for breast cancer depends largely on:

A. Her personal preference

B. Her weight

C. Where she lives

15. The last time you or a member of your family faced a serious illness, where did you turn first to get information?

A. A medical dictionary

B. The Internet

C. Your doctor

16. You have a problem. Your child has been admitted to an Ivy League college and a second-tier college. But the second-tier college has offered a much more generous financial aid package, and you aren't sure you can swing the cost of an Ivy. What do you do?

A. Take the more generous aid offer.

B. Send your child to the better school, and borrow to the hilt.

C. Call the Ivy League school and negotiate for more aid.

17. Given the opportunity to save some money, most consumers would change their electricity provider without a second thought.

    A. True

    B. False

18. Which of the following best describes your attitude at work?

    A. I keep my head down, do whatever I'm asked, and try to keep my boss happy. I'd like to keep this job until I retire.

    B. I get my work done and go home. A job's a job. If a better one came along, I'd take it in a minute.

    C. I treat my job as a place to learn something that will be useful in my next job.

19. When it comes time to sell some of the stocks or mutual funds in your portfolio, which are you most inclined to do?

    A. Sell the stocks with big capital gains, to lock-in profits.

    B. Sell the stocks that have lost money.

20. If you believe in the New Economy, you can feel confident that the stock market isn't overvalued.

    A. True

    B. False

21. To make a fortune in business, it's more important that you start with:

    A. Some seed capital

    B. A good idea

22. *Which best describes your view of retirement?*

    A. It's not something I need to worry about until I'm older.

    B. My money is all tied up in my house; I'll sell it and move to a smaller one when I retire.

    C. I never plan to retire completely; I'd like to keep working as long as I'm able.

    D. I put away a certain amount of money every month for retirement.

23. *Which better describes your attitude toward using a credit card?*

    A. I'll use it in a store or restaurant, but I never give it out over the Internet.

    B. I use it in stores, restaurants, and on the Internet.

24. *When you get an unwanted telemarketing call during dinner, do you:*

    A. Hang up immediately?

    B. Politely say "No thank you" and hang up?

    C. Curse and hang up?

    D. Listen to the pitch?

    E. Demand to be put on the company's "No call" list?

25. *Do you usually fill out the product registration card when you buy a new product?*

    A. Yes

    B. No

Scoring

Question 1. If you answered:

A or B, give yourself 5 points. At least you've got the right idea.

C, give yourself 10 points.

D, zero.

Question 2. If you answered:

A or B, give yourself 5 points.

C, give yourself 15 points.

D, zero.

Question 3. If you answered:

A, subtract 5 points. You think inflation is going to help you "grow into" that mortgage? Forget it. Your head's in the past.

B, zero.

C, give yourself 5 points.

D, give yourself 10 points.

E, give yourself 15 points.

Question 4. If you answered:

A, subtract 5 points.

B, add 10 points.

Question 5. If you answered:

A, zero points.

B, add 10 points.

If you don't know what an Internet fare search service is, subtract 5.

Question 6. If you answered:

A, way off. Zero.

B, getting closer. 5 points.

C, bingo. 10 points.

Question 7. If you answered:

A, You're suffering from "inflation illusion." Zero.

B, You understand the value of lower inflation. Give yourself 5 points.

Question 8. If you answered:

A, zero. Only 12 percent of mutual fund managers beat the market in 1998.

B, 10 points. You're catching on.

Question 9. If you answered:

A, zero. Inflation was higher in 1992, and the *real* (after inflation) wage increase was smaller.

B, 5 points.

Question 10. If you answered:

A, zero.

B, give yourself 5 points. In the network world, many products—software, for instance—are worth more if they are used by more people.

Question 11. If you answered:

A, subtract 5 points. You're like most people, but often these different versions are just an effort to get you to pay more.

B, subtract 10 points. The New Economy will eat you alive.

C, add 5 points.

Question 12. *If you answered:*

A, subtract 5 points. Hotels often maintain a variety of discount rates that, with a little cajoling, can be yours.

B, add 5 points.

Question 13. *If you answered:*

A, subtract 5 points. Medical research shows that those who do it most, tend to do it best.

B, add 5 points.

C, zero. Nice thought, but hospital infection rates aren't publicly available (although they should be).

Question 14. *If you answered:*

A or B, zero.

C, add 5 points. Health care standards in the United States vary enormously by region.

Question 15. *If you answered:*

A, add 5.

B, add 10.

C, zero.

Question 16. *If you answered:*

A, zero.

B, add 5.

C, add 10.

Question 17. *If you answered:*

A, zero.

B, add 5. Experience in Pennsylvania and California shows most consumers are reluctant to switch, even if it saves them money.

Question 18. *If you answered:*

A, subtract 5.

B, zero

C, add 5.

Question 19. *If you answered:*

A, zero. Like most people, you prefer to avoid taking losses. But the strategy also means you often sell better stocks than the ones you keep. And the tax laws treat you more kindly if you sell the losers.

B, add 5.

Question 20. *If you answered:*

A, zero.

B, add 5. Even in the New Economy, human nature will eventually lead investors to overvalue the market.

Question 21. *If you answered:*

A, zero.

B, add 5.

Question 22. *If you answered:*

A or B, subtract 5.

C, add 5.

D, add 10.

Question 23. If you answered:

A, subtract 5. With encryption, your credit card information is safer on the Internet than it is in a store or restaurant.

B, add 5.

Question 24. If you answered:

A, B, C, or D, zero.

E, add 5.

Question 25. If you answered:

A, zero.

B, add 5. Product registration cards are usually just an attempt to get you to provide personal information, which may be sold to others.

3

A Personal Journey to the New Economy

I graduated from the University of North Carolina in 1977 with a degree in English literature and without ever stepping foot in an economics course. But economics intrigued me. The U.S. economy wasn't doing well at the time. Inflation had taken hold, President Gerald Ford's "Whip Inflation Now" buttons notwithstanding, and growth had faltered. I thought economics might be a useful window for a young journalist trying to understand all this, and I began asking around about graduate programs that would teach economic principles to a humanist.

Saul Friedman, a journalist whose lectures I attended at nearby Duke University, recommended I look into the New School for Social Research in New York. I knew little about the school, except that it was home to Robert Heilbroner, the author of a popular little book on the great economists, *The Worldly Philosophers*, which, whatever its economic merits, was gracefully written.

On a spring day after graduation, I drove my Toyota station

Key Dates
in the New
Economy

April 1974
Intel intro-
duces the
8080 chip, the
brains of the
first personal
computer,
with 6,000
transistors.

33

wagon up the New Jersey Turnpike into lower Manhattan and straight to the New School. I didn't have an appointment, but I went to the office of the director of admissions and explained my mission to the woman at the front desk.

"There's a southern boy here who thinks he wants to study economics," she shouted loudly into the director's office.

January 1975 The first personal computer, the Altair 8800, is released by Micro Instrumentation and Telemetry Systems and featured on the cover of *Popular Electronics*.

"Does he have an appointment?" the director shouted back.

"No," she said.

"Then send him right in."

I could see the look of anguish on the face of the student beside me, who apparently *did* have an appointment. But I took the invitation and went in.

"Would you like a cup of coffee?" the director asked.

"Yes, please," I replied.

"Well, you'll have to get it yourself. My secretary's a Marxist. She doesn't get coffee."

"That's all right. I don't need coffee." I retreated.

"Now," he continued, "why do you want to study economics? You were on track with your English studies. We have a fine degree program here called a masters in liberal studies. You could write your thesis on James Agee. He's from down there where you're from. Wonderful writer."

After a short lecture on Agee and his beginnings in the New Deal's Work Projects Administration, the director finally consented, with reluctance, to arrange a tour of the school by someone familiar with the economics program. It was then I learned I had entered my father's nightmare: Seven of the eight members of the New School economics faculty were avowed socialists. The eighth was Heilbroner.

I didn't attend the New School, but my visit there said something about the state of American economic thinking in 1977. The New School was a unique institution, but it wasn't totally aberrant. In 1977, much of the American intelligentsia was still ambivalent about the great battle between capitalism and communism. At the University of Chicago, a strong strain of classic free-market liberalism was taking hold, fueled by the works of Friedrich von Hayek and Milton Friedman. But elsewhere, there was still a feeling among many academics that the Cold War would lead, not to victory for one side or the other, but to a new synthesis, a third way. The Scandinavian countries, Sweden in particular, were seen as models by some, with government planning and harnessing private industry.

November 12, 1975
Microsoft is founded.

Recently, I reread one of the most popular and influential economics books of the day, *The New Industrial State* by John Kenneth Galbraith. It is still an interesting critique of the American economy circa 1970 and a revealing window into the thinking of the time. But it could not have been more wrong about where the U.S. economy was headed.

Galbraith's view was that the giant American corporations—General Motors, ITT, General Electric—were "no longer subordinate to the market." Instead they had become giant bureaucracies that were creating and planning the market. They would decide months, or even years, in advance what products were to be made; they would organize their resources to manufacture those products; and then they would advertise to make sure consumers bought the products that had been manufactured.

April 1, 1976
Apple Computer is founded in Steve Job's bedroom (not his garage).

The upshot: "We have an economic system which, whatever its formal ideological billing, is in substantial part a planned economy," Galbraith wrote. "The initiative in deciding what is to be produced comes not from the sovereign consumer who, through the market, issues the instructions that bend the productive mechanism to his ultimate will. Rather it comes from the great producing organization which reaches forward to control the customer to its needs."

Galbraith saw this American-style, corporation-planned economy as surprisingly similar to the Soviet-style, government-planned economy. "In time, and perhaps in less time than may be imagined," he wrote, convergence "will dispose of the notion of inevitable conflict based on irreconcilable difference."

The most surprising part of Galbraith's thesis, in retrospect, was his argument that this drift toward a planned economy was being forced by *technology*. Advanced technology, he said, required a task such as the manufacture of a car to be subdivided into many component parts, so technology could be applied to each part. That in turn required companies to operate on a huge scale, investing large amounts of capital and operating with long lead times. Marshalling capital and resources over such long periods of time required *planning*. Technology, in Galbraith's view, didn't work in favor of a consumer-driven free market; it worked directly against it.

How wrong he was.

That spring day, as I drove out of Manhattan, the seeds of the revolution were being planted. A man by the name of Alfred Kahn, a Cornell University professor who headed the New York Public Service Commission, had gotten a call from the White House asking if he would agree to head the Civil Aeronautics Board, the government agency that regulated airplane schedules and fares. He declined, saying he would prefer to head the Federal Communications Commission, which regulated the phone company, an area in which he had some expertise. He knew nothing about airlines.

November 1976 Jimmy Carter is elected president.

October 1978 The Airline Deregulation Act of 1978 is enacted.

In the subsequent days, however, Kahn did some research. And what he discovered was that an unusual political consensus was forming in Washington about airline regulation. The Civil Aeronautics Board had been started during the 1930s. It was intended to ensure reliable service and low rates for customers. But instead of benefiting consumers, regulation mainly seemed to be protecting inefficient and poorly run airlines. Some unlikely people were beginning to join the call for deregulation of the airlines, including Senator Ted Kennedy of Massachusetts, who at the time was being advised by a lawyer named Stephen Breyer, now an associate justice on the Supreme Court.

April 1979 Harvard professor Ezra Vogel writes *Japan as Number One: Lessons for America.*

Mr. Kahn was a follower of Thorstein Veblen, the great satirical writer and economist whose work *The Theory of the Leisure Class* was as skeptical as Galbraith's of the ability of the free market to deliver the greatest happiness to the most people. But Kahn was also a realist. And after looking into the matter, he agreed that airline regulation was hurting the consumer, not helping.

A few days later the White House called again: "The president wants to see you." Alfred Kahn went to Washington and met with President Jimmy Carter in the Oval Office. The president "made it quite clear that he thought this was where the action was going to be," Kahn told me twenty years later. The professor accepted. He asked one of the president's advisers if the president understood that deregulation meant that "either Eastern Airlines or Pan Am is going to go belly up." "He understands" came the reply.

May 4, 1979 Margaret Thatcher becomes prime minister of England.

Kahn went on to rid the airline industry of the regulations that had defined service and held up prices since the New Deal. At first he moved slowly; but he soon concluded that gradual deregulation was impossible, and the entire regulatory regime was lifted. His prediction proved more than true: both Eastern Airlines and Pan American Airlines shut down. But deregulation also turned America into a nation of fliers. Airline fares dropped by a third over the next two decades, according to a study by the Brookings Institution. And the number of airline passengers in the United States rose from 275 million in 1978 to 614 million in 1998.

July 15, 1979
President
Carter diag-
noses na-
tional
"malaise."

The Beginnings of the Network

As the seeds of deregulation were being planted in Washington, an important breakthrough in the building of a global computer network was happening in Cambridge, Massachusetts.

Three scientists at the MIT Laboratory for Computer Science were working on a puzzle. They were trying to devise a mathematic formula that would allow people to freely exchange digital documents without having to worry about the documents' being intercepted and read. After months of effort, they thought they had a solution, based on the factoring of very large numbers. Their breakthrough was published in the August 1977 edition of *Scientific American.*

The article caused shock waves in Washington. The government provided most of the funding for the MIT lab. And intelligence officials were alarmed, fearing such a public discussion of cryptologic matters might harm their intelligence-gathering efforts.

The director of the National Security Agency, Admiral Bobby Inman, summoned the director of the computer lab, Michael Dertouzos, for a meeting. In the interest of academic freedom, Dertouzos refused to agree to the notion that MIT should seek government permission before publishing such papers. All he promised was to send the government early copies of the papers, giving officials the opportunity to initiate legal proceedings if they felt a need to attempt to prevent publication.

The meeting marked an important turning point. Up to that time, the development of leading-edge computer technology had occurred under the auspices of the government's defense establishment. But now, leading-edge computer technology was moving out of the government's hands, into the public domain.

Dertouzos had grown up in Athens, Greece. "I was a crazy kid," he told me, "the kind who puts sails on his bike and jumps out of second-story windows with two umbrellas."

He had spent hours wandering through the giant Athens flea market, swapping information and gossip and buying electronic parts for his inventions. "I spent every Sunday there," he recalls. "It was unbelievable. Prices could vary by 1,000 percent. I learned to haggle. You could find anything you wanted, negotiate, and buy."

In 1964, Dertouzos came to MIT and began working on one of the world's first "time-shared" computers at the Laboratory for Computer Science. The entire operation was a creation of the U.S. Department of Defense, which in the wake of the Soviet Union's surprise launch of the Sputnik satellite in 1957, had created the Advanced Research Projects Agency. ARPA chose MIT and Stanford and Carnegie Mellon universities as the front lines for its research into time-shared computers.

His first year on campus, Dertouzos attended an after-dinner speech in which a top ARPA official, J. C. R. Licklider, laid out his view of a future in which computers and people would act in concert. Most of the scientists in the room, he recalls, rolled their eyes.

But ARPA created the Arpanet, a computer network that allowed computer scientists at twenty universities and a few military

August 6, 1979 Paul Volcker becomes chairman of the Federal Reserve Board.

sites to share research and even play games together. One game involved several players in remote locations who were given ten randomly chosen letters on their computer screens and three minutes to create as many English words as they could. Each time a player composed a successful word, it showed up simultaneously on every player's screen, giving the originator credit. Nonsense words were rejected by the computer. It was one of the world's first interactive digital games.

October 6, 1979 Fed chairman Paul Volcker switches to targeting monetary aggregates; interest rates soar.

Dertouzos became director of the computer lab in 1972. In 1980, he gave a speech in Washington at a technical conference, where he laid out a prescient vision of an information marketplace, modeled on the Athens flea market of his youth.

By the year 2000, he imagined:

> The toy personal computers of the early 1980s have become useful and powerful machines owned by small businesses and by many individuals. . . . A wealth of private and public networks interconnect all of the machines, which number in the ten millions. Entrepreneurs and a new breed of information companies offer a variety of legal, financial, medical, recreational, educational and government information services for a fee. Many traditional ways of doing business have changed. For example, advertising is done in reverse, by a service that responds to consumer inquiries with products and services that match.

Dertouzos had come to understand what Galbraith didn't: that technology would not lead to centralization and bureaucracy. Instead, it would lead to the exact opposite. It was a democratizing force that would decentralize power and flatten bureaucracy. The central development was an "ongoing, relentless improvement" in the performance, size, and cost of both memory and processing computer chips, and the remarkable advances in communications technology, particularly satellite communication and laser-driven fiber optic communications.

To many, Dertouzos's speech sounded like pure science fiction. But in retrospect, it was one of the earliest clarions heralding the world to come.

November 1979 Tokyo Round of trade talks is completed.

Margaret Thatcher's Revolution

After my trip to the New School, I put aside plans for graduate school, returned to Tennessee, and went to work for *The Chattanooga Times*. While there, I took evening courses in economics at the local university and read, cover to cover, Paul Samuelson's *Principles of Economics*—which at that time made generous references to Galbraith's *The New Industrial State*. After two years, I headed off to the London School of Economics to pursue a master's degree.

I arrived in London in the summer of 1979, just a few months after Margaret Thatcher had taken over as prime minister. Like the Democrats in America, the Labour Party in England had seen the handwriting on the wall and had already begun grudging movement away from the welfare state. Denis Healey, Labour's finance minister, had adopted a policy of monetarism—the tough, anti-inflation prescription of the conservative Milton Friedman. But it was Thatcher—the Iron Lady, as the Russians called her—who came to embody the free-market revolution.

Unlike her most recent conservative predecessors, Thatcher was certain, stubborn, and uncompromising. Stories buzzed about

Whitehall of her shutting up ministers in the presence of visiting officials. While recession made her task exceedingly difficult in the early years, she knew where she wanted to lead the country. She was for a tight monetary policy to rein in inflation; cuts in welfare and government spending; a shift away from income taxes, which she argued destroyed incentives to work and invest, to a value-added tax, which encouraged savings; and privatization.

November 4, 1979
Iranian students take hostages at U.S. embassy.

Most important, she saw the Cold War as a struggle between right and wrong. And she was determined that Britain be in the right.

None of this had sunk in with the student body at the London School of Economics in the fall of 1979. Their knowledge of Thatcherism came only from the sharp cuts in student subsidies the government had enacted. The school at that time was a magnet for students from every corner of the globe, and they didn't appreciate having their generous funding cut.

The University of North Carolina had been a sunny place of blue skies, budding dogwoods, and bright-faced girls in colorful, hand-knitted sweaters who could coax three or four syllables out of a simple "Hi!" Intellectual pursuits and social pursuits were in constant competition. Politics didn't have a chance.

November 4, 1980
Ronald Reagan is elected president.

But on the gray, grassless, urban campus of the London School of Economics, politics was everything. And in spite of Thatcher's election, most of the politics tilted precipitously to the left. The spectrum of political clubs began with a very small Labour Party group and shot off into the ether from there. One of the clubs appeared, from the flyers it posted on the walls, to be exclusively devoted to the cause of diplomatic recognition for Albania. Three others gathered each year to celebrate the birthday of Joseph Stalin. (I'm not making this up.)

The year I was in London was also the year that Iranian students took over the U.S. embassy in Tehran and held its occupants hostage. The elected head of the student body of the London School of Economics sent a letter to the Iranian students saying he supported their bold actions.

But in the midst of this cauldron of radicalism was an economics program still stubbornly devoted to the study of the classical free market economy. The school had been home in the 1930s and 1940s to Hayek, who later moved to the University of Chicago and whose book *The Road to Serfdom* marked the early beginnings of the turn from the welfare state and central planning and back toward a decentralized free-market system.

The icon of the program was a large, lumbering gentleman with flowing white hair—Lord Lionel Robbins—whose career in public life had peaked around 1930 and who afterwards had repeatedly crossed swords with John Maynard Keynes at Cambridge. I attended his lectures on the history of economic thought, which, about halfway through the course, turned into a series of fascinating first-hand reminiscences. Like monks copying Renaissance texts to preserve them through the dark ages, Lord Robbins and his colleagues at the school had clung to their elegant studies of the classical free-market economy throughout the twentieth century.

The Japanese Model?

I returned to Washington in the summer of 1980, just in time to witness the revolution at home: the election of Ronald Reagan as pres-

May 21, 1981
U.S. prime interest rate peaks at 20.5 percent.

July 1981
Recession begins in the United States.

ident. I took a job on a weekly magazine, the *Congressional Quarterly.*

On election night, I watched the returns with my future wife, Lori Esposito. She worked for the U.S. Arms Control and Disarmament Agency and knew that if elected, Reagan planned to shut down all arms control negotiations with the Soviet Union and thus end her employment. But she had grown weary of Jimmy Carter and was ready for a change.

August 13, 1981 Reagan locks out the air traffic controllers, breaking the strike.

Reagan was a sunnier version of Margaret Thatcher. She was the stern headmistress; he was the cheerleader. And his version of Thatcherism had a peculiar, feel-good twist, which came to be known as supply-side economics. Its centerpiece was a huge tax cut, which had been brought to the new president courtesy of an unusual trio of characters. There was Arthur Laffer, a bubbly but erratic economist who had encountered controversy in Washington and scorn in academia; Jude Wanniski, a messianic journalist who befriended Laffer and popularized a curve he had drawn on a napkin suggesting that at some point higher tax rates might mean less government revenue; and Jack Kemp, the former-football-player-turned-congressman, who seized on the Laffer-Wanniski formulation to advocate across-the-board income tax cuts. Unlike the stern Thatcher, they saw no need to ruin a good thing by making up for lost revenue with a value-added tax.

August 1981 Reagan tax cut passes Congress.

The Republican Party had embraced Kemp's tax cut in the 1978 mid-term elections, and Ronald Reagan climbed on board in his 1980 campaign. To help counter the view that tax cuts would lead to giant deficits, the Reagan team trotted out an economic wise man, Alan Greenspan, who attested that the numbers added up. Later, of course, as chairman of the Federal Reserve, Greenspan would rail against the budget deficits that followed.

Tax cuts came to define the Reagan agenda. But Ronald Reagan's overriding goal was no different from Margaret Thatcher's—to reduce the influence of government in society. Like Mrs. Thatcher, he saw the Cold War as a battle between right and wrong. And he had no doubts about who was right.

August 1981 IBM introduces the IBM PC.

In the face of Reagan's victory, and later his immense popularity, talk of Galbraithian-style "planning" disappeared from American political discourse. But the search for a third way, between capitalism and socialism, didn't stop. Instead, it shifted its attention across the Pacific to Japan, which was racking up an impressive economic record. In 1979, the respected Harvard University professor Ezra Vogel published *Japan as Number One: Lessons for America.* In the United States, it was a bestseller; in Japan, it went off the charts.

Curious, I decided to go to Japan. I applied for a Henry Luce Scholarship, which provided a year working in Asia for young Americans who had no academic background in Asian studies—a standard of ignorance I easily met. I was given a spot in Tokyo at the *Nihon Keizai Shimbun,* Japan's leading business daily, and I used that perch to explore the mysteries of the Japanese economy and society.

January 8, 1982 Justice Department drops thirteen-year-old antitrust case against IBM.

Economic science made no distinctions among peoples, but I was struck in Japan by how fundamentally different the people were. Americans and Europeans bore some resemblance to the economic man of the academic models, aggressively pursuing their self-interest and asserting their rights. But the Japanese I met seemed caught up in an intricate web of obligations that sometimes oddly limited their pursuit of self-interest.

A simple example could be seen at the store where I shopped. On weekends, the clerks would offer free samples of food to shoppers. My Western friends seldom declined them; but the Japanese seldom accepted them. The gift, they feared, would carry with it an unwanted obligation, perhaps to buy.

November 1982 Recession ends in the United States.

A young American I met in Tokyo was employed as an engineer by a small Japanese firm—at the time, a rare circumstance. The company had invited him to Japan immediately after his college graduation, given him a two-year contract, then showered him with benefits, hoping to make him feel indebted to the company and thus obliged to stay when his two-year contract expired. The American accepted all these benefits, taking days off while his colleagues were working, and even asked for more. Yet he had no intention of staying. "If they don't want me to do these things, they shouldn't let me," he said, American-style. "I've told them where I stand."

It was clear to me that the Japanese economy was far from the ideal of free, flexible, and competitive markets I had learned about in school. Consumers were given low interest rates on their savings deposits and had few alternatives for investment. The flow of capital was not free, but directed, both by the powerful Ministry of Finance and by the giant business groupings, or *keiretsu,* each of which included a bank that favored lending to other companies in the group. Labor markets were inflexible: large companies found it difficult or impossible to get rid of employees, employers were reluctant to hire workers who had worked for competitors, and employees felt tied to one company for life. Antitrust laws, though modeled in the postwar era after U.S. laws, were only lukewarmly enforced. Many of the giant export manufacturers were awesomely productive, efficient, and competitive; but service industries and the entire distribution system of the country were just as awesomely inefficient. Trying to open a bank account at a Japanese bank in 1982 was such a daunting task that I eventually gave up.

Watching typesetters at the *Nihon Keizai Shimbun* turn the handwritten notes of journalists into computerized copy also raised questions about how Japan would fit into the coming technological revolution. Japanese reporters wrote their stories with pencils, and typesetters then transferred the stories to computer by pointing to some two thousand different characters on a giant, computerized chart. The Japanese language was clearly going to be a disadvantage in the new world of computers.

January 1983 *Time* magazine names the personal computer "Machine of the Year."

The political scientist Chalmers Johnson published a book that year, *MITI and the Japanese Miracle,* in which he argued that government policy was responsible for Japan's stunning economic success. He said the Japanese, relying on an intelligent and elite corps of bureaucrats and united in their acceptance of economic development as the preeminent goal, had constructed an industrial policy that was outperforming more purely market-based systems. And many in the United States at that time were inclined to believe him.

But I was skeptical of Johnson's argument, and puzzled. "While the common wisdom concerning Japan is that government protection and support has caused industry to flourish," I wrote in my final report to the Luce Foundation, "the common wisdom concerning the U.S. and other Western economies is that government protection and support causes industry to grow fat and atrophy." How could both be right?

It was a question that continued to be debated for another decade and a half. The Japanese economy collapsed at the beginning of the 1990s, but other Asian countries that had followed the Japanese model of development continued to skyrocket.

Then, in 1997, came the Asian financial crisis. The clubby financial systems that had once been seen as a source of "long-term" investment were fingered as culprits. "Crony capitalism" became the new term. And Deputy Treasury Secretary Lawrence Summers shuttled about Asia—like a "new MacArthur," said the German analyst Stephen Gotz-Richter—urging Asian nations to rebuild their financial systems in the American image.

January 1, 1984   AT&T is broken up.

For a story I was writing at the time, I called Jeffrey Garten, dean of the Yale School of Management, who was one of many who had praised the Japanese financial system, in his 1992 book *Cold Peace*. "I certainly made some misjudgments about the strength of the Japanese system," he acknowledged.

"These very long-term, living-together relationships misallocate capital," Rudi Dornbusch, an MIT economist, said more bluntly.

Warming to Milton Friedman

I came home from Japan in 1982, put in another year at the *Congressional Quarterly,* then got an unexpected call from Al Hunt, who had just become Washington bureau chief at *The Wall Street Journal.* He needed an economics reporter and wanted to know if I was available. I'll always be grateful for that opportunity and for the many things Al Hunt did for me over the next decade.

At the *Journal,* I was assigned to what my friends called the "up-down" beat. I would write stories off government press releases about how durable goods orders went up or new home sales went down. Those stories quickly became second nature for me. I would dash them off in the morning, then have the afternoon free to pursue other topics of interest.

In late 1985, I was given an assignment to write about the brightest lights in academic economics and how they were grappling with the problem of persistently high unemployment. I quizzed the academic economists I knew and came up with three people: George Akerlof at the University of California at Berkeley, Joseph Stiglitz at Princeton, and Lawrence Summers, who was then at Harvard. Akerlof and his wife, Janet Yellen, had team-taught my macroeconomics course during their two-year stay at the London School of Economics, and Yellen later became a member of the Federal Reserve Board of Governors and chair of President Bill Clinton's Council of Economic Advisers. Stiglitz later served as chairman of the Clinton council, before becoming chief economist at the World Bank.

January 24, 1984 Apple Computer introduces the Macintosh with Orwellian Super Bowl ad in which a female runner throws a sledgehammer through image of Big Brother.

And Summers, then only thirty, became a friend and, eventually, secretary of the treasury. He was the clearest-minded economist I knew and was a master at applying complicated theoretical concepts to real-life situations.

At the time, Akerlof, Stiglitz, and Summers were all working in the Keynesian tradition, trying to find coherent explanations for why the invisible hand of Adam Smith, the seventeenth-century economist, wasn't working the way it was supposed to. In the classical model, high unemployment leads to lower wages, which in turn cause more workers to be hired and unemployment to fall. But in 1985, after three years of strong economic expansion, unemployment remained a stubborn 7 percent.

The three men theorized one reason for that might be what they called the "efficiency wage theory." The theory suggested companies

49

might pay workers more than the market required in order to elicit higher productivity, or perhaps to reduce the costs of searching for the best workers. As a result, the invisible hand would break down, with wages staying too high and unemployment staying high as well.

November 6, 1984
Reagan is re-elected.

Summers wrote that an "industrial policy" of subsidizing high-wage firms might be one way of addressing such a problem. But he, too, had grown skeptical of government-led solutions and was quick to add that such policies could present "practical" problems. "Policy is always several years behind theory," he told me at the time, "and it's a damn good thing it is."

More than a decade later, after becoming a top official in the Clinton administration, Summers discussed how his views on the economy had changed over time in an interview with the author Daniel Yergin for Yergin's book *The Commanding Heights*. Refer-ring to Milton Friedman, the godfather of modern free-market economics, Summers, whose parents are both distinguished econo-mists, said: "He was the devil figure in my youth. Only with time have I come to have large amounts of grudging respect. And, with time, increasingly ungrudging respect."

In 1986, I spent much of my time covering the tax reform bill, with my colleague Jeffrey Birnbaum. Later, we told the bill's Perils-of-Pauline story in our book *Showdown at Gucci Gulch: Lawmakers, Lobbyists, and the Unlikely Triumph of Tax Reform*. Following that bill provided an education in the ways of Washington. And in the end, it also gave me a new faith in the flexibility and adaptability of U.S. political institutions. The tax reformers had taken on legions of special interest groups, each with a huge stake in one or more of the $300 billion worth of targeted exemptions, credits, and deductions that the bill slated for elimination. But in the end the special interests lost, and the reformers won.

At the end of the book, we wrote:

> Tax reform was a uniquely American idea—that somehow the nation could start over and rebuild its entire tax system. "No other country would try anything like this, to go back to the beginning, to be born again," said Aaron Wildavsky, a political scientist at the University of California at Berkeley. "It was quite a radical proposal."

March 11, 1985
Mikhail Gorbachev takes power in U.S.S.R.

In 1980, Tibor Scitovsky, the head of the American Economic Association, had warned members of the association at their annual convention that modern economies were in danger of a kind of sclerosis, or hardening, that would work against free-market forces. The hardening would be caused by the expanding role of government, by the growing power of large corporations, by labor unions, and by a proliferation of government "incentives" and favors demanded by special interests. "Capitalism works when it's flexible, but self-destructs when it is not," Scitovsky said.

But by the mid-eighties, evidence was beginning to accumulate that the trend Scitovsky commented on was turning around. The U.S. economy was remaking itself, becoming more flexible, more supple, more susceptible to market forces than ever.

The Fall of the Wall

In December of 1989, I traveled to Poland with a group of businessmen and top government officials sent on an economic mission by President George Bush. The Communist Party had just fallen in

Poland; Solidarity had taken the reins. And now the Poles and a throng of well-wishers around the world were grappling for the first time with the question of how to transform a communist economy into a capitalist one.

It wasn't going to be easy. Behind the Iron Curtain, industry had developed with a peculiar logic, unlike anything known in the West. Enterprises had no notion of profit or cost, and their methods were hopelessly outdated. We visited an electronics factory that was considered one of the best in the country—and found vacuum tubes in use.

Except for some beautiful cut crystal, there was little being made in Poland that would sell in the West at any price. The new labor minister, Jacek Kuron, candidly told his U.S. counterpart, Labor Secretary Elizabeth Dole, that over the next few years, as much as half of the workforce would probably have to find new jobs.

How to manage that transition? Some imagined a gradual change that would cushion the blow. Others thought Poland's union-led government could pioneer a new, more worker-friendly form of capitalism, perhaps looking to Scandinavia, or Asia, for its model. Given the opportunity to start over, the Poles could meld the social ideals of the socialist state with the efficiency of the capitalist state. They could find a third way.

But when the American delegation met with the new finance minister, Leszek Balcerowicz, they learned he had no doubts about his course. "We don't want to try a third way," he said bluntly, much to my surprise as I stood with a small group of reporters in the back of the room. As for the notion that Poland should meld socialism and capitalism, he rejected it outright. "We have had enough experiments here. Let wealthier countries experiment." His plan was to

May 24, 1985 Quantum Computer Services, the precursor to America Online, is created.

November 1985 Microsoft introduces Windows software.

slash subsidies in half, decontrol prices, and drastically reduce the budget deficit. If a million Poles were forced into unemployment as a result, so be it.

Even the American businessmen who heard his message had their breath taken away. The big question on their minds, Barry Sullivan, chairman of the First National Bank of Chicago, said, was this: "Will this prove to be an act of monumental courage? Or sheer folly?"

September 1986 Tax reform bill passed by Congress.

The most surprising thing about the collapse of communism was that it was so complete. Few of those who had been living behind the Iron Curtain felt any nostalgia for what they were leaving behind. Few talked about "saving the best" of the old system to meld with the new. There was no Galbraithian convergence, no synthesis. Communism had lost; capitalism had won.

I once heard Hedrick Smith, who had covered the old Soviet Union for *The New York Times,* recount a joke he had heard in Russia at the time of communism's collapse. Three men gathered in front of Lucas Cranach's famous painting of Adam and Eve, naked in the Garden of Eden. The first, who was British, speculated that the two people were British, since in no other society would a man and a woman share an apple in such a civilized way. The second, who was French, said the figures in the painting were French, since in no other society would a woman give her body to a man for merely an apple.

January 8, 1987 Dow Jones industrial average reaches 2000.

But the third man, a Russian, said Adam and Eve were obviously Russian: they had no clothes, no shelter, only a single apple to eat between them—and someone had told them they were in paradise. The great Marxist experiment of the twentieth century had ended in total humiliation.

In the United States, there were still many who worried about the weaknesses of American-style capitalism. Earlier in 1989, the historian Paul Kennedy had published a book, *The Rise and Fall of the Great Powers,* which suggested the United States was caught up in the inevitable process of decline that eventually afflicted all great nations. Even President Bush's own treasury secretary, Nicholas Brady, shared the concern of many at the time that U.S. capital markets were forcing U.S. companies to pay excessive attention to quarterly earnings, and thus discouraged them from making the long-term investments that were helping Japanese companies take the lead.

March 1987
Bill Gates's net worth hits a billion dollars.

But men like Balcerowicz spent no time worrying about the shortcomings of American-style capitalism. They had tasted communism. And they saw only one way out.

As Westerners began to get a closer look behind the Iron Curtain, the reasons became clear. The communist economies were basket cases—far worse than ever indicated by the statistics that U.S. intelligence agencies had used to justify Cold War defense budgets. Galbraith's theories notwithstanding, the giant enterprises east of the Iron Curtain could not begin to play in the same league with those in the West.

July 1987
Allied Signal chairman Edward Hennessy explodes over 39 percent rise in company health care costs; demands managed care.

I got a firsthand look at that problem in September 1991, when I accompanied a group of American money managers to Russia, led by Dean LeBaron of Batterymarch Financial Management in Boston. Included in the group were the manager of General Motors' $34 billion pension fund, the manager of New Jersey's $28 billion pension fund, and a money manager of a U.S. insurance company with more than $250 billion in assets. Their goal was to see if some of the defense industries of the former Soviet Union might be a worthy place to invest a small piece of their enormous pools of capital. The defense establishment, they reasoned, was the pride of the Soviet system; these businesses, long shielded from Western view for security reasons, might provide the beginnings of a turn-around in Russia.

Our first stop was Zelenograd. This, we were told, was the Silicon Valley of Russia. It didn't look like Palo Alto. There were high-rise apartments with corrugated metal balconies, women in soiled scarves, men in baggy suits, and a twenty-foot bronze statue of Lenin watching over the scene. Inside, our guide insisted, lies "practically all the intellectual power in the Soviet Union in the field of microelectronics."

August 11, 1987 Alan Greenspan succeeds Paul Volcker as Fed chairman.

Outside the director's office, a secretary sat with nine different-colored phones crowding her desk. Why so many phones? I asked. The answer: Here in the Soviet Silicon Valley, there are still no multiline phones.

We were taken into a giant conference room once used to brief Soviet generals on the latest missile technology. A huge metal chandelier hung over the table, with a third of its bulbs burned out. On the wall, a giant red star bore the logo "The October Revolution."

A man in a gray suit and a gray tie gestured at hand-drawn charts with a wooden pointer. He quickly conceded that Zelenograd makes nothing that would interest the affluent countries of the West. But, he gamely insisted: "Our products will be competitive in the Third World." The economics of capitalism hadn't yet sunk in: why would anyone buy Russian integrated circuits, when they lag decades behind their Western counterparts in both cost and quality?

October 19, 1987 Black Monday: Dow drops 508 points.

Someone at the table circulated a popular Russian joke of the time: Russia makes "the largest microprocessors and the fastest watches in the world."

In Moscow, a large exhibit hall displayed the defense industries' efforts at transformation. There was a refrigerator made by an old cartridge factory; clocks and watches made in a plant designed for mechanical bomb fuses; sewing machines, exercise machines, disco lights. There was even a crude "boom box" made in a former radio-fuse factory.

January 1989 Paul Kennedy publishes *The Rise and Fall of the Great Powers*, suggesting U.S. power has peaked.

"It's not a Sony," said Vadim Sintsov, whose title—director of main administration for international economic relations in the ministry of defense industry of the U.S.S.R.—reflected the nation's regard for efficiency. "But still, it's good for the Russian buyer because it is in rubles." No one could tell us how many man-hours it took to make any of these products; such things weren't measured in Russia. And no one could tell us where we could buy them. A visit to the GUM department store later that day found little but empty shelves. Later, Mr. Sintsov conceded that the wait for a new refrigerator was three years.

Another joke circulating Moscow at the time told of the man who is informed his new car will be delivered to him on May 16 in the year 2003. "Could you make it in the afternoon?" he replies. "I have a plumber coming that morning."

The Cold War had ended in complete and unequivocal victory for the West. Capitalism worked; communism didn't. Margaret Thatcher and Ronald Reagan had gotten their wish. There was no third way. And the implications of that victory would prove to be just as earthshaking in the West as the implications of defeat were in the East.

Within ten years, the last remnants of communism were gone

and, with them, much of the faith that Western nations had once put in government solutions to economic problems. In the United States, in particular, an almost mystical faith in the power of private markets took hold. States contracted with private companies to handle their welfare systems; the Postal Service had to compete with Federal Express; roads were built and operated by private companies. In the post–Cold War economies, society's willingness to rely on free markets and private solutions to once-public problems reached heights unimaginable only two decades earlier.

April 10, **1989** Intel introduces the 486 chip, with 1.2 million transistors.

Greenspan's Economy

When I joined the *Journal* as an economics reporter in 1983, I was given a list of "business economists"—a distinct breed from academic economists. They were the people who made a living by evaluating the current state of the economy for businesses and investors and who paid attention to the numbers that came out of the government's statistics mills each day. More to the point, they were the people I could call for quotes to adorn my stories on durable goods orders or inventory-to-sales ratios.

I soon learned who I could rely on, and I divided those into two groups. There were the quote-meisters, an extremely useful breed, always quick to take my phone calls and always willing to give a pithy comment to support the thesis I was developing that day. Then there were the people I would seek out when I was genuinely confused about an economic indicator, perplexed by its importance, and wondering what it really said about the economy's direction.

The second list was very short. At the top was Alan Greenspan.

Greenspan never made it easy. If he sensed I had already developed a point of view, he would invariably argue against it. And even

57

before he became a central banker, his syntax was, well, Greenspan-ian. Reporters live for good quotes. My favorite from the days of writing about economic indicators came from Lawrence Chimerine, who, when asked why the latest numbers didn't comport with his forecast, replied, "I don't know. Maybe I should just give up and become a hockey goalie." Greenspan never would have said that.

June 1989
Tianamen
Square mas-
sacre takes
place in
China.

But Alan Greenspan, I learned, had his finger on the pulse of the economy like no one else alive. He would burrow into the statistics, parse them fifteen different ways, and tell you exactly what they were saying. He was smart, he was thorough, and he was wise. He had both knowledge and experience. I learned to call on him whenever I felt deeply confused about what was happening in our economy and was in need of guidance. Greenspan, in turn, tolerated my questioning and nagging with both patience and humor. I ran into him on an airplane the day my former teacher, Janet Yellen, was named by the Clinton administration to the Federal Reserve Board. "She taught me everything I know about economics," I told him. "That's the worst thing I've heard about her yet," he replied.

Cautious by nature, Alan Greenspan certainly wasn't the first to recognize that a historic convergence of political and technological forces was going to completely change our economy. Others can vie for that honor. Edward Yardeni, the chief economist at Deutsche Morgan Grenfell, can certainly claim to have jumped quickly on the trend. As early as 1990, Yardeni wrote an article entitled "The Triumph of Adam Smith." In 1993, he forecast that the high-tech revolution would lead to a surge in productivity. And in October 1996 he came out with an early paper predicting the Internet would become "a global auction market" that would hold down prices for consumers and have extraordinary consequences for the economy.

But what Greenspan brought to the argument was a depth of understanding and analysis that no one else could bring. To this day, he hedges his words carefully. "I do not say we are in a new era, because I have experienced too many alleged new eras in my lifetime that have come and gone," he told a conference at the Federal Reserve Bank of Chicago in May 1999. Nevertheless, he has clearly become convinced we are in a period of economic energy unlike any seen in a century.

November 9, 1989 Berlin Wall collapses.

For Greenspan, the analysis starts with business inventories, an area in which he specialized as a consultant. In the old economy, manufacturers never knew for sure when the next load of sheet metal might come in, or when customer demand might surge or fall off. As a result, they kept large inventories to hedge against delivery risks.

"Most twentieth-century business decision making has been hampered by dated and incomplete information about customer preferences in markets and flows of materials through a company's production system," he said in his Chicago speech. In this respect, his analysis of the old economy is somewhat similar to Galbraith's. Unable to get timely market signals, manufacturers are forced to *plan* rather than respond to the market.

But in the new economy, information is pervasive. The manufacturer can get instant information about the latest movement in demand for its products and has tracking systems that will tell exactly when the next order of sheet metal will come in. Inventories can be scaled back or even eliminated; so, too, can entire layers of the distribution chain. And the production process, now largely computerized, can adapt almost instantly to any changes.

Robert Parry, long-time president of the Federal Reserve Bank of San Francisco, gave me one of the most vivid examples of how this process works in practice. He visited a lumber mill in his district—a low-tech industry if there ever was one. But this mill used lasers to analyze each log before it was milled and then used a computer program to decide instantly how to cut each log *on the basis of real-time information about the current market price for each cut*. If there was a shortage of four-by-fours, that information would be indicated by a price rise and the mill would cut more four-by-fours. Market signals were immediately transferred back to the very beginning of the economic chain.

And it's not just *how* things are produced that distinguishes the New Economy; it's also the *things* that are produced. Here's how Greenspan put this in his Harvard commencement address in June of 1999:

> The quintessential manifestations of America's industrial might earlier this century—large steel mills, auto assembly plants, petrochemical complexes, and skyscrapers—have been replaced by a gross domestic product that has been downsized as ideas have replaced physical bulk and effort as creators of value. Today, economic value is best symbolized by exceedingly complex, miniaturized integrated circuits and the ideas—the software—that utilize them. Most of what we currently perceive as value and wealth is intellectual and impalpable.

In Greenspan's view, and now many others' as well, the powerful forces of globalization, deregulation, and digitization are remaking the American economy, from beginning to end. No industry is left

December 29, 1989
Japanese stock market peaks, with Nikkei at 38,916.

July 1990
Recession begins in the United States.

untouched. The changes are as thorough and as profound as those that swept through the economy in the early half of the nineteenth century, when the Industrial Revolution was taking hold.

The New Economy

So what is the New Economy?

The term is sufficiently vague that it can encompass many different ideas for many different people. Canadian economist Nuala Beck was one of the first to use the term, and even registered it as a trademark. Her 1992 book *Shifting Gears* focused on the role technology is playing in remaking the economy. As mentioned above, deregulation, privatization, globalization, and the collapse of communism also all play a role.

But perhaps it's best to define the New Economy by its effects:

October–December 1990 Tim Berners-Lee creates the World Wide Web.

In the New Economy, recessions seem less likely—although certainly not impossible

In the old economy, inventories had a lot to do with economic cycles. When times were good, businesses tended to assume they would stay good. If demand for products dropped for some reason, businesses would be slow to find out about it. They would continue manufacturing, perhaps for months, building up a bulge of inventories. Finally, the message would get through. Then they would shut down factories and sell off their bulging inventories. If this happened on an economy-wide scale, a recession could result.

In the New Economy, however, manufacturers have real-time information on demand for their products. If demand changes,

December 9, 1990 Lech Walesa, former Gdansk shipyard electrician and founder of Solidarity, is elected president of Poland.

they respond. Inventories are unlikely to build up unintentionally; as a result, recessions may be less likely to occur.

In the New Economy, inflation seems to have a harder time taking hold

April 17, 1991 Dow reaches 3000.

In the long run, inflation is a monetary phenomenon. It happens, as Milton Friedman has long argued, when an economy has too much money chasing too few goods. But in the short run—and the short run can last for many years—the story is much more complicated.

In the old economy, labor unions could force prices up by demanding higher wages. Big companies in oligopolistic industries could raise their prices as well, and their few competitors would follow. While customers might not like price increases, they often had little alternative but to go along.

In the New Economy, few have that kind of pricing power. Labor unions have lost their hold—the percentage of private company employees who are unionized dropped from 21.5 percent in 1975 to just 9.5 percent in 1999. And most companies face much more vigorous competition, both globally and at home.

Because the things of value in today's economy are much lighter, and because capitalism now spans the globe, products manufactured everywhere can quickly be shipped anywhere, by plane or in cyberspace. If one company raises prices, there's likely to be another one somewhere else willing to take over its business at the lower price. And new information technology, particularly the Internet, makes it easier for customers to comparison-shop and find the best prices. Inflation is still possible, but it has a much harder time taking hold.

In the New Economy, unemployment can be lower

Until a very few years ago, most economists thought that there was a "natural rate of unemployment" of about 6 or 6.5 percent. If unemployment fell below that level, theory held—and experience suggested the theory was true—companies would have to bid up wages, higher wages would lead to higher prices, and inflation would result.

But unemployment broke the 6 percent barrier in August 1994, then fell below 5 percent in July 1997, and kept falling, without sparking inflation. Had Alan Greenspan not understood what was happening in today's economy, he might well have raised interest rates in order to stop the precipitous fall of joblessness. Instead, he conducted a grand experiment, ignoring conventional economic wisdom and defying the Fed's own internal predictions that inflation would result.

March 1991
Recession ends in the United States.

Most important, the New Economy means rising wages and standards of living

The convergence of a more competitive business environment and huge leaps in technology means companies both can and *must* become more efficient. They need to do more with less, in order to compete. As a result, the value the average worker can create— known as the *productivity* of that worker—is rising. Over time, as productivity rises, wages will also rise, and living standards as well.

During the first twenty-five years after World War II, productivity in this country rose at a brisk 2.7 percent a year. During that quarter century, American living standards doubled as new families filled new homes with appliances and put one or even two cars in the garage.

But since 1973, productivity growth has been much slower—barely 1 percent a year, on average. At that pace, it would take seventy years for living standards to double. Economists have marveled at how productivity growth could remain low, in spite of the rising use of computers. "You can see the computer age everywhere these days except in the productivity statistics," Nobel economist Robert Solow once observed.

In the last couple of years, however, the New Economy has finally begun to show itself in the productivity figures. Since 1996, the numbers have risen at rates greater than 2 percent. My *Wall Street Journal* colleagues Bob Davis and David Wessel give a compelling argument why that rise is likely to continue in their book *Prosperity: The Coming 20-Year Boom and What It Means to You.* While some naysayers, like the Northwestern University economist Robert Gordon, still question whether the change is lasting, their argument has gotten increasingly difficult to sustain.

The impact of rising productivity is profound. Wessel and Davis use a simple example to illustrate it. If productivity growth remains at 1 percent, a typical married couple will see their income grow from around $49,700 in 1996 to around $60,650 twenty years later, ignoring the effects of inflation. If productivity growth is a half percent higher, you put another $6,000 in their pocket twenty years hence. To a middle-class family, that small change in productivity means a lot of money.

A more dynamic and competitive economy, of course, has its costs. Companies and workers alike find the landscape shifting quickly beneath them. The economist Joseph Schumpeter aptly called the process "creative destruction." Indeed, one theory for why inflation has remained low is that workers fear the New Economy

December 25, 1991 Gorbachev steps down, and the Communist Party collapses.

February 7, 1992 Maastricht Treaty signed calling for common European currency.

may make their job skills obsolete and are, consequently, less willing to push for pay increases.

Moreover, the New Economy may mean greater inequality in pay and income. Since 1973, the share of income going to the most affluent fifth of the population has risen a sharp 22 percent, while the share going to the least affluent has dropped 6 percent. Social conventions in the old economy helped key pay levels from varying too greatly. But in the New Economy, pay is driven by the market. Sports stars, movie celebrities, and corporate chief executives can see their market values rise to many millions of dollars, while unskilled workers with little education must compete for work against the low-paid workers in underdeveloped countries.

August 18, 1992 Japanese stock market bottoms out, with Nikkei at 14,309, down more than 60 percent from peak.

Eventually, though, a rising tide will lift all boats. If productivity growth goes back to the rates of the 1950s and 1960s, those at the bottom of the income scale will benefit. And indeed, in the last few years, there have been encouraging signs that pay for those at the bottom is rising faster than that for the rest of the population.

The Internet Economy

Changes in the economy are reducing the risk of recession, lowering levels of unemployment and inflation, and raising living standards. But that's only part of the story. The New Economy is also dramatically changing the inner workings of the economy. Thanks largely to technology, the whole intricate structure of our system of business and commerce is being radically transformed.

November 3, 1992 Bill Clinton elected president.

Steve Case had a notion twenty years ago of what the future would look like. When he applied for a job at the J. Walter Thompson advertising agency in 1980, the *Journal*'s Kara Swisher recounts in her book *AOL.COM,* he wrote:

I firmly believe the technological advances in communication are on the verge of significantly altering our life. . . . Innovations in telecommunications (especially two-way systems) will result in our television sets (big screen, of course!) becoming an information line, newspaper, school, computer, referendum machine, and catalog.

May 27, 1993
Clinton budget passes
Congress.

What neither Case nor anyone who knew him imagined at the time, or for many years to come, was that he would become a titan in that world, opening a door for millions of Americans to the Internet.

Case was turned down by the Thompson agency. He worked for a brief period as an assistant brand manager for Procter & Gamble, marketing a wipe-on hair conditioner ("Towlette, you bet!" was the slogan). Then he worked briefly developing new toppings for Pizza Hut.

He entered the online world in 1983, joining Control Video Corporation, the tiny forerunner of America Online. The firm was always an underdog, first battling companies funded by giants of the old economy like General Electric, then facing the giant of the New

March 22, 1993 Intel introduces the Pentium chip, with 3.1 million transistors.

Economy, Microsoft. His company was forever plagued by public predictions of its demise. When Case told my colleague Walt Mossberg in 1991 that his struggling firm would soon be the largest online service in the world, Mossberg was incredulous. But Case was right.

I went to visit Case at his company's sprawling—and still growing—campus in Sterling, Virginia, to hear his vision of where the wired world is leading. AOL's mission, posted on a wall in the entryway, is to create a "medium as pervasive as the telephone or television." But it's clear Case believes the Internet will have a greater effect on society than the telephone or television. Soon, it will be a network connecting not just computers, but televisions, cell phones, palm computers, and, eventually, automobiles, home appliances, and just about anything else that can be embedded with a microchip.

"Through many types of devices, networks will become more of an anytime, anywhere, all the time, everywhere environment," Case says. "Interactive services will be embedded in everyday life.

"If the majority of people get connected"—something he expects to happen by 2003 or 2004—"and when they are connected all the time, it will put the consumer in charge in ways that weren't really possible before. They can get the information they want, when they want, the way they want, on topics they care about. They'll be able to learn more about products and services before they make a purchase decision, and to research the price.

"It will give them more perfect information in a more perfect market."

Case understands, better than many of his tech competitors, that this vision both fascinates people and frightens them. "Consumers are on the one hand intrigued by these possibilities, but on the other hand terrified by the complexity that it might bring on," he says. "Consumers will need help integrating this into their lives, keeping it simple, keeping it affordable."

That's exactly what America Online plans to do: present the new technology "on a silver platter." And that's exactly why the company has thrived, in the face of countless predictions of its demise. Some technology prophets had predicted that the New Economy would mean death to the middleman, since the network can directly link producers and consumers. But in fact, the New Economy is giving rise to a new sort of middleman—a middleman focused on the

September 1993 National Center for Supercomputing Applications releases beta version of the Mosaic web browser.

November 20, 1993 NAFTA treaty is approved by Congress.

needs of consumers instead of the needs of producers, a middleman who can help consumers organize and simplify their lives. America Online is a leading example.

One sign that this new world is maturing is the fact that it no longer resides principally in Silicon Valley. The frontiers are being pushed forward in Case's northern Virginia home, as well as in Cambridge, Massachusetts; Austin, Texas; Raleigh, North Carolina; Santa Fe, New Mexico; and countless other places.

One of the most creative minds in the new Internet world is Jay Walker, who works in Stamford, Connecticut, in the shadow of corporate headquarters of the old economy. Walker has a picture of Thomas Edison hanging on his wall and fancies himself an Edison for the Internet age. His company, Walker Digital, "invents" Internet business plans and then travels to Washington and seeks to patent them at the U.S. Patent Office. He has applied for no fewer than 250 patents.

"In the old economy, there was a hierarchical, unidirectional flow of commerce," he explained when I went to visit him. That's the world Galbraith described: giant corporations, like Procter & Gamble, deciding what to produce, then producing it, distributing it, and marketing it to unsuspecting consumers.

"But in the New Economy, there is a multidirectional network flow of commerce. Buyers are sellers; sellers are buyers; everybody is everywhere."

To get a glimpse of what Walker means, you have only to look at his most successful invention to date: Priceline.com. On Priceline, the world of Procter & Gamble is turned upside down. The transaction starts with the consumer. If you are buying an airplane ticket,

April 4, 1994
Jim Clark and Marc Andreessen found Mosaic Communications Corp., the precursor of Netscape Communications Corp.

you say where you want to go *and you say what you are willing to pay.* Airlines with vacant seats then bid for your business.

The Priceline example demonstrates why the Internet has the potential to radically change market economics. Even back in Adam Smith's day, markets were less about products than they were about information. How is the farmer to know which crops to grow? How does the pin maker know how many pins are needed? How does the consumer communicate the fact that he or she has plenty of pots and pans, but not enough blankets? The market provides answers to those questions. If consumers need more blankets than pots, they will pay more for blankets. And as prices for blankets rise, more people will make blankets and fewer will make pots.

April 15, 1994 Final act of the Uruguay Round trade negotiations is signed in Marrakesh, creating the World Trade Organization (WTO).

The Internet allows that signaling to become far subtler, far more intricate, far more complete, and far faster. In the old economy, Procter & Gamble presented you with a product at a price and you could take it or leave it. If you took it, they would keep making it; if you left it, the brand would be discontinued.

In the New Economy, however, you can signal what Walker calls "latent" demand. I *might* be willing to buy that product if you changed it in this way, or I *would* be willing to fly on your airplane if you lowered the price by $50. That kind of detailed signaling was never possible before.

Like Case, Walker believes we are just at the very beginning of this revolution. "The child is only six or seven years old," he says.

One big breakthrough on the horizon, he believes, will come when voice recognition software takes hold—"when a guy can talk to his television." That's when the Internet will break the final barrier, becoming "more pervasive than electric power."

To take the vision a step further, I traveled a few hours farther up the East Coast to Cambridge, where Michael Dertouzos continued to seek the limits of the new world. In his book *What Will Be,* he imagines the modern version of a mall. It has no products, just a collection of cubicles outfitted with video screens, special goggles, and instrumented gloves. Put them on, and you can see yourself in new clothes, and order them custom-fitted to your body. Or you can test drive a new car, choosing options as you go along. The goggles make the virtual experience almost like the real thing, and the gloves allow you to "feel" the things you want to buy.

This is not science fiction. The technology exists, and it is practical. In fact, it may be more practical than the construction of sprawling malls filled with millions of dollars of idle inventory.

Computer magnate Michael Dell has shown the potential in this new world for what's become known as "mass customization." The visitor to his website can actually construct his or her own computer before purchasing it. I've started visiting a website called ShirtCreations.com, which lets me make my own shirts—choose fabric, cuffs, collars, buttons, and sizes to the quarter inch. The shirts are expensive—about $100 each—but that will soon change. With computers, mass customization can be less expensive than the old and costly method of holding huge, premanufactured inventories.

I had a cup of coffee recently with a northern Virginia entrepreneur named Raul Fernandez, who once worked for Jack Kemp but now heads a firm, Proxicom, that is helping businesses figure out the potential of e-commerce. Fernandez was talking to General Motors about a plan to leapfrog Internet car-buying services like Auto-by-Tel and allow car buyers to customize their cars, Michael

April 26–29, 1994   First all-race elections take place in South Africa.

August 1994 Al Dunlap lays off one third of the employees of Scott Paper Co., earning him the sobriquet "Chainsaw Al."

Dell–style, over the Internet. The technology for manufacturing customized cars already exists at GM, he says. The remaining problems are logistical and political: how to get the customized car to the purchaser and how to keep the network of local car dealers happy in the process.

The above examples all deal with the consumer products business, which is just a slice of the big picture. Dertouzos imagines a man hurt while on vacation in Alaska who hooks up to a hospital kiosk and has his vital signs read by a doctor at home, or perhaps has a chest X ray sent to a specialist in Minneapolis, all in a matter of minutes. Or a banker in Arizona who is laid off, but applies via an Internet broker for banking openings across the country. She interviews for the job online and ends up working for a new international bank that allows her to work from home.

> November 8, 1994 Republican Party picks up 52 seats in the House, 8 seats in the Senate, and bicameral control of Congress for the first time in forty-two years.

These are not wild musings; they are happening.

The New Economics

How will an "anytime, anywhere, all the time, everywhere" network change the rules of economics? So far in this book, I've stressed how the New Economy marks a return to the free-market vision of Adam Smith. It puts power in the hands of consumers by (1) vastly expanding their choices; (2) vastly increasing the abundance, quality, and usefulness of the information they have at their disposal; and (3) forcing businesses to compete to please them.

> February 23, 1995 Dow reaches 4000.

But there are important characteristics of the New Economy that carry at least the potential to turn Smith's vision into a jumble.

First, there is the issue of scarcity. Open any basic economics textbook, and that will be one of the first words you encounter. In Greg Mankiw's 1998 *Principles of Economics,* it is in paragraph four, boldfaced. "Economics is the study of how society manages its scarce resources," Mankiw writes.

But networks often obliterate scarcity. They make information ubiquitous—like air. A great novel or a brilliant new piece of software may be costly to create; but once created, it can be reproduced and distributed to millions, even billions, at little or no cost.

October
1995 11
percent of the
adult popula-
tion of the
U.S. and
Canada say
they've gone
online in the
last month.

In Adam Smith's economy, the more people who consume a good, the less value it has to each. If ten of us share the same bicycle, its value to each of us falls sharply. If a hundred share it, the bicycle becomes all but useless.

But in the network economy, it's often true that *the more people who use a product or service, the more valuable it becomes.* When Alexander Graham Bell and his assistant Thomas Watson were the only ones connected to the telephone line, that line wasn't particularly useful. But as more and more people became connected, the value of the telephone network vastly increased.

In the New Economy, there are more and more products and services that are subject to such network economics. I'm using Microsoft Word software to write this book, but not because I like it. I

November
21, 1995
Dow reaches
5,000.

find it unnecessarily complex and annoying. In fact, I find myself cursing Microsoft Word the way my father used to curse our Pontiac station wagon. At times in the course of writing this book, the software has mysteriously decided to change the typeface or the format of certain paragraphs, forcing me to laboriously change it back. It seems to have a mind of its own. (If it's really smart, it'll excise this paragraph altogether.)

Still, I use Microsoft Word because I know all my coworkers use it and my publisher uses it. The fact that it is so prevalent makes it more valuable to me than any more elegant, but less common, alternative.

Network economics creates some problems for Smith's invisible hand, many of which have to do with pricing.

First, there's the question of whether to charge a price at all. Air is one of the most valuable commodities on the planet, but because it is ubiquitous, no entrepreneur has yet figured out a way to extract a price for its use. A similar phenomenon can already be seen spreading on the Internet.

My former colleague in San Francisco, George Anders, recently wrote a story about a company called E-greetings Network Inc. The company tried to sell e-mail birthday cards for 50¢ to $2.50 a piece. Then it decided to cut the price to zero, hoping to make up the difference on advertising and sales of other, less virtual products like flowers and candy.

"Charging for cards was a small idea," the chief executive of the firm boldly told Anders. "Giving them away is a really big idea." Indeed.

"Plenty of other fast-growing companies are committing similar forms of pricing suicide in cyberspace," writes Anders, "and then declaring they have cleared their path to success. Want to receive a fax? Open an Internet account? Collect your voice mail, make a long-distance call, listen to music or read commentary by prominent writers? No-cost versions of all these services are popping up on the Internet, to the consternation of established rivals that believe in charging for their services."

The Internet guru Kevin Kelly encourages business to join this *free* free-for-all. In his book *New Rules for the New Economy,* he

> **February 1996** Telecommunications Act is passed, deregulating telecommunications companies.

> **October 14, 1996** Dow reaches 6,000.

writes: "Because prices move inexorably toward the free, the best move in the network economy is to anticipate this cheapness."

Kelly argues that in the New Economy, the only truly scarce resource is human attention. He quotes Nobel laureate Herbert Simon, who says: "What information consumes is rather obvious: It consumes the attention of its recipients. Hence a wealth of information creates a poverty of attention."

November 5, 1996 Bill Clinton is re-elected.

Heeding Simon's dictum, Internet companies are now scrambling to compete for human attention—or what aficionados call "eyeballs." Whoever has the most eyeballs, the current wisdom holds, will win the contest.

In early 1999, I heard Kelly and others discussing this concept at the annual meeting, in the snow-blanketed mountain town of Davos, Switzerland, of the World Economic Forum, a gathering of supposedly wise folk. One of the hot Internet start-ups at the time was Buy.com, which claimed it was going to win the competition for eyeballs by selling products at a price *below their cost.* Eventually, it would make money by selling advertising or referring customers to other commerce sites.

February 1997 Scottish scientists successfully clone a sheep named Dolly.

Perplexed, I stood to ask a question: "As a newspaperman, I have learned to appreciate the money that comes from advertising. But can we all survive on advertising?" The answer: No one yet knows for sure. But here's a disconcerting fact: Of the $4 billion spent on Internet advertising in 1999, just ten companies garnered 75 percent of it. Everyone else was fighting for leftovers.

Sell it? Or give it away? The debate is playing out in the newspaper business. Rich Jaroslovsky, who used to be an editor in the *Journal*'s Washington bureau, has become something of a celebrity in the Internet world. He edits the paper's interactive edition, which is the only online newspaper that has succeeded in getting hundreds of thousands of people to pay for the service.

The New York Times, on the other hand, now boasts some seven million registered users on its free site. The *Journal* believes it has bested the *Times* by getting subscribers to pay; the *Times* believes it has beaten the *Journal* in the battle for eyeballs. At this early stage, who can say who's right?

February 13, 1997 Dow reaches 7,000.

While businesses are trying to figure it out, consumers can enjoy an abundance of free products and services on the web. But in the long run, the answer could have enormous implications for the American economy.

Even if a company decides to charge for an information product, there is still the question of how much to charge. The economics textbooks say that in a competitive economy, prices will settle at the point where "marginal cost" equals "marginal revenue." If it costs $100 to make one more widget, then a widget company will be willing to sell as many widgets as it can at that price, or just above it, since the extra money is profit. If the company tries to charge too much, another widget maker will come along and steal the sale.

But for many information products, such as software, the fixed costs of making a product can be quite high, while the marginal cost—the cost of giving it to one more person—is low, or even zero. If they followed textbook pricing, software companies would quickly go out of business.

May 2, 1997 Tony Blair, champion of "The Third Way," takes power as prime minister in Britain.

This, of course, isn't new; many companies face the same problem. Pharmaceutical companies are one example. Inventing an important new drug can be a very costly business, while manufacturing a drug often costs only pennies. Airlines are another. Buying a plane, stocking it with fuel, and getting it into the air is costly. But the cost of letting one more customer take an empty seat can be as low as $20.

The government helps solve the drug maker's problem by granting it a patent and thus temporarily shielding it from competition so it can set its own price. That enables the company to charge higher prices for a while, in order to recoup its investment. Such temporary monopolies for "intellectual property" will become more prevalent in the New Economy. But the government will have to exercise caution; if patents and copyrights are issued too freely, the consumer will lose the benefits of competition. Some argue that's already happened in the pharmaceutical industry, where life-saving drugs may be priced out of the reach of many needy patients.

July 16, 1997
Dow reaches
8,000.

The airlines offer another interesting example. Textbook pricing would drive them out of business. But high prices increase the likelihood that their planes will fly with empty seats, leaving profits on the table. In response, they have learned to master the art of *price discrimination.* If you have to leave on short notice and don't want to stay over Saturday night, the airlines will charge you the highest rates, figuring you are a business traveler who's willing to pay. If you're staying for a weekend and booking in advance, the airlines bet you're a leisure traveler, who won't fly without a lower fare.

August 1997
Microsoft in-
vests $150
million in
Apple.

On the Internet, more and more companies are learning to raise price discrimination to a fine art, as have the airlines. In their book *Information Rules,* Carl Shapiro and Hal Varian of the University of California at Berkeley business school, coach companies on how to do this. One tactic they teach: versioning. Create a "deluxe" version of your software, for instance, for people who are willing to pay more and a "standard" for those who aren't.

This, of course, is a tactic practiced in the old economy as well.

But a Toyota Lexus costs more to make than a Corolla. In the New Economy, say Shapiro and Varian, software companies often make the deluxe version first, then spend extra money to take away some of its functions to create a low-cost model to sell.

Microsoft, for instance, offered Windows NT Workstation for about $260 and Windows NT Server for $730 to $1,080, according to Varian and Shapiro. But analysts found the software to be essentially the same. With modest tuning, the low-end product could be turned into a high-end product. IBM used a similar tactic with its LaserPrinters, the authors say. The cheaper LaserPrinter Series E was functionally equivalent to the standard LaserPrinter, but half as fast. A consumer testing lab found a chip had been inserted to intentionally slow down the printer, so IBM could divide its market.

Here's another trick that Shapiro and Varian urge Internet companies to use. Instead of offering just two versions of a product, try three. Research shows many consumers who pick the low-priced option when given just two choices will choose a higher, medium-priced option if they have three choices. "Consumers try to avoid extreme options," the authors say. They suggest calling the low-price option "standard," the middle option "professional," and the high option "gold."

This a crude approach, compared to what's coming. The Internet sends information in both directions, and thus gives new power to the buyer and the seller. As Internet companies learn more about you and your specific buying habits, they'll tailor appeals directly to you, priced at levels they believe you're willing to pay. If you've happily paid high prices or shown a preference for "deluxe" versions in your Internet shopping, then they'll pitch you only their highest-priced products. But if your neighbor has been an aggressive price

April 6, 1998
Dow reaches 9,000.

May 18, 1998
Justice Department files broad antitrust suit against Microsoft.

shopper on the web, they may offer him or her virtually the same products at a deep discount.

The Importance of Brands

Adam Smith's famous treatise used the example of a pin factory to describe how a competitive economy works. But pins are something you can see and feel. You can judge the quality of the pin *before* you buy one.

November 24, 1998 AOL and Netscape announce merger plans.

In the New Economy, the products and services you buy can't be judged for quality in advance. When you decide to enter a restaurant you've never been in before, to see a new movie, to buy a new suite of software, or to sign up with a new health service, you are buying into an unknown. There's a substantial risk involved; the food may be lousy, the movie boring, the software buggy, the health service poor. For the consumer, that can create a lot of uncertainty.

One way the New Economy reduces that uncertainty is by providing an endless stream of information. You can read reviews of the restaurant, the movie, the software, and you can even see how the health service is rated by its own customers.

December 19, 1998 Bill Clinton is impeached by House.

But another way the New Economy addresses consumers' uncertainty is with branding. If the restaurant is McDonald's, the movie is made by Disney, the software is developed by Microsoft, or the health service is the Mayo Clinic, you can feel more confident about the nature of the product or service you are about to buy. Brands reduce uncertainty for consumers. They take some of the risk out of life. They make things simpler. And in an increasingly complex world, where human attention is the scarcest resource, simplicity is often what people are looking for.

There was a time when many economists thought brands interfered with the workings of a market economy. Brand names and brand name advertising, they thought, led consumers to perceive differences that don't really exist. Why should people pay more for Procter & Gamble's soap, they argued, when an identical soap is sitting on the shelf next to it at a lower price? The economist Edward Chamberlin once even proposed that the government discourage branding by refusing to enforce the exclusive trademarks that companies use to identify their products.

But in the New Economy, brands are becoming more important than ever. That's in large part because they simplify the increasingly complex decisions consumers are called on to make. Maybe there's a better running shoe to be found than Nike, but I'll buy Nike because I know that such a big and prominent company can't afford to make a truly bad shoe. Maybe that restaurant will have better food than McDonald's, but maybe it won't, and at least with McDonald's I know what I'm getting. Maybe someone else will sell me the book I need more cheaply than Amazon.com, but I know Amazon provides good service. Brands are decision-making shortcuts; and in a world demanding that consumers make ever-more decisions, shortcuts are welcomed and embraced.

For business, the real challenge of the New Economy is getting the attention of consumers. Consumers hold all the power; but they also have limited time and a lot of competing demands for their attention. Brand names are one way to capture their attention.

Entertainment is another. Indeed, it's no surprise in the New Economy that entertainment and commerce gradually seem to be merging. If you doubt that, visit the Mall of America in Minneapo-

January 1, 1999 The Euro, the new European currency, is introduced.

February 12, 1999 Bill Clinton is acquitted by the Senate.

lis. Is it a shopping mall? Or a theme park? In a world where businesses must compete for the consumer's attention, entertainment becomes ever more important.

America Online, Yahoo, and the other Internet portals have come to recognize that; their websites must be fun as well as useful. Advertisers know it too; a simple banner ad at the top of a website won't get anyone's attention. Instead, you have to lure the web surfer in with the promise of entertainment.

Today's successful businesses "have to create an experience" for the consumer, writes business consultant Michael J. Wolf in a book entitled *The Entertainment Economy.*

> They have to inform and amuse; they have to build a destination. In other words, just as shoppers have come to expect milk producers to add vitamin D to their product, consumers are looking for the E-Factor in every product—that's E as in Entertainment. It's an extremely effective way of standing out from the rest of the pack. And only if a company's product stands out is someone going to pick it off the shelf or off the Web site on the Net.

The traditional economist may balk at that notion. When you walk into a store to buy shoes, shouldn't you be thinking about the quality and price of those shoes—not whether basketball superstar Michael Jordan wore them in a television ad?

But the New Economy is about serving consumers' wants and desires. And those wants and desires aren't always rational. For those who want the best quality shoe at the lowest possible price, the New Economy provides the means to find it and buy it. But for

March 29, 1999 Dow reaches 10,000.

April 1999 40 percent of the adult population of the U.S. and Canada say they've gone online in the last month.

those who would rather spend a little extra money to enjoy a connection with their favorite sports hero, well, the New Economy offers that as well. Your choice.

The Problems of Scale

In the economics textbooks, goods or services that can be extended to new customers at no cost are called "natural monopolies." Mankiw's book uses the fire department as an example. Since fires are rare but the firemen must be on guard at all times anyway, it costs nothing to add one more house to a protected neighborhood. Before deregulation, telephones and electric utilities were also seen as "natural" monopolies. The cost of wiring one more house was low compared to the high fixed cost of building the switching or generating stations.

May 3, 1999
Dow reaches
11,000.

Today, the term "natural monopoly" has fallen out of favor in the public debate, as faith in private markets has grown. In the past, natural monopolies were put under regulation; and regulation, as in the case of airlines, often worked to the detriment of the consumer. According to the new conventional wisdom, it's almost always considered better to rely on private markets than on regulation.

But the natural monopoly concept has new applications in the New Economy, since so many businesses fit the textbook definition. They can expand at little cost, and they gain benefits from getting ever more people onto the same network, so there's a natural inclination to grow. Big is better. And as a result, the New Economy is increasingly characterized by what many call a "winner-take-all" phenomenon. Once one company emerges as the clear leader in a business, customers move to it, "tipping" it toward monopoly. That's what happened in the battle between Sony betamax and VHS

July 1999
Bill Gates's
net worth
reaches $100
billion.

formats for home videos. And it's why Microsoft now supplies the operating system for almost every computer sold.

The danger for consumers in this arrangement is that once winning companies have driven their competition out of business, they may start raising prices or else lose their drive to innovate. Technology optimists say that's nothing to worry about; if the market leaders get complacent, a new competitor, or even a new technology, will come along and take their business. Thus, they say, the phone companies now have to worry about competition from cable, satellite, and cellular; and Microsoft has to worry about America Online. "There will be a series of temporary concentrations that are quickly overthrown by another concentration," predicts Kevin Kelly.

August 2, 1999 Intel introduces the Pentium III chip, with 9.5 million transistors.

But others are less confident that the new world won't eventually lead to a group of new behemoths, like the robber barons of a century ago.

One man in the middle of this debate is Joel Klein, the assistant secretary for antitrust in the Department of Justice, and the man who sued Microsoft. Klein didn't ask for the job; his real hope was to be named solicitor general, which would give him a chance to argue before the Supreme Court—a lawyer's dream. But the antitrust job has given him a peculiar window on the New Economy. "I happen to be here at a terrific time in history," he says.

It's also a paradoxical time. On the one hand, competition appears more robust than ever before, with consumers reaping the benefits. On the other, given the dynamics of the New Economy, the tendency of one company to dominate its market may be greater than ever.

Klein makes clear that monopoly alone is not a concern for his office. "Amazon.com, e-Bay, nothing keeps them in their leading position except good service, good prices, or good marketing" he says. The consumer benefits as a result. More troublesome is when monopolies gain control over bottlenecks that allow them to restrain competition. The computer operating system could be one such bottleneck, he fears; set-top boxes could be another.

Inevitably, Klein says, "we are going to see the accretion of market power. And then the question will be, what do companies do to extend that power?" If they violate antitrust laws, he says, the government must be prepared to intervene. "Left alone, people will get market power and abuse it." As a result, Klein believes, vigorous antitrust enforcement will be critical to keeping the New Economy competitive in the future.

It's been nearly 230 years since Adam Smith penned his classic description of how people pursuing their own self-interest would "be led by an invisible hand to promote" the greatest good for society. Today, the basic insights of that classic work seem, in some ways, more valid than ever. But as Bradford De Long and Michael Froomkin point out in a recent paper on the subject, the "microeconomics of the Invisible Hand fray badly when transported to the information economy."

The New Economy is clearly going to call for some new economics.

November 5, 1999 Judge Thomas Penfield Jackson finds Microsoft wields monopoly power in PC operating systems.

January 10, 2000 America Online announces it will purchase Time Warner in the mega-merger of the New Economy.

4

Shopping in the New Economy

The Consumer Reigns

While living in London, I sometimes browsed the rare-book stores in nearby Leicester Square. I bought a collection of old books, including a vintage edition of Adam Smith's *The Wealth of Nations,* as well as first editions of Hayek's *The Road to Serfdom* and Galbraith's *The New Industrial State.*

At some point, I decided that I'd like to add a copy of Samuel Johnson's classic eighteenth-century *Dictionary* to my collection. From that time on, whenever I saw a used-book store, I wandered in to see if they had the *Dictionary.* I searched for two decades, in bookstores in Washington, New York, London, Tokyo, and even in rural Maine and Tennessee. I once found a rare first edition, but it cost thousands of dollars, so I continued my search in hopes of finding something less expensive.

Then one evening, I took my quest to the Internet.

In about an hour's time, with the help of barnesandnoble.com, I had scoured used-book stores from Martinez, California, to New Preston, Connecticut, and found more than a dozen different editions of Mr. Johnson's great work, in varying conditions. Publix Books in Cleveland Heights, Ohio, had a first edition selling for $12,250. Heritage Book Shop in Los Angeles had a second edition for $9,375.

I finally settled on a copy of the tenth edition, published in 1792, which was available at Northshire Bookstore in Manchester Center, Vermont. The book was described as being in "very good" condition, with "warm, nicely worn old leather boards" and "faint yellowing" of the pages. It was listed for $600.

Eager for human contact before laying down my money, I called the bookstore. They confirmed the book's existence and its condition and offered to sell it for $500—$100 less than the online price. I sent a check, and two weeks later, the book was in my collection.

I enjoyed my two-decade search for this book, probably more than I will enjoy the book itself. I was happy to have an excuse to wander into musty old shops and purposefully peruse their rare-book collections. The old economy had its pleasures.

But my evening's book excursion on the Internet showed how much the world had changed. Geography has lost its meaning in commerce. Leicester Square has no advantage over Manchester Center. My ability to choose had increased at least a hundredfold.

The New Economy is a buyer's world. The three great trends of our time—globalization, deregulation, and digitization—have given the consumer more choices and more information than ever before. And choices and information mean market power. Twentieth-century economists have long taught the notion of consumer sovereignty; but only in recent years have consumers experienced its full force.

The two central economic questions facing society have always been these: What goods and services will be produced? And how will they be distributed? Throughout history, those questions have been answered in many ways. In some early societies, a single leader made the key economic decisions; in others, a council of elders. In medieval times, kings and feudal lords had power over both production and distribution.

But the world that Adam Smith described more than two hundred years ago put that power in the hands of consumers. The market was a kind of early network, allowing consumers to signal their desires and their buying power. The information was passed on to others by way of prices. If a merchant tried to raise the price of his pots, consumers could take their business to the next stall and let the high-priced merchant go out of business. But if the price of all pots began to rise, then the pot makers knew the time had come to make more pots.

The Industrial Revolution, however, eventually wreaked havoc with Adam Smith's market. Mass production of ever more complicated products meant decisions often had to be made about what to produce, and in what quantities, long before the product went to market. The price-signaling system, which worked so beautifully in the increasingly elaborate models being built by economists, began to break down in actual practice—most spectacularly during the Great Depression. The invisible hand froze up, and the economy plunged into years of high unemployment and slow growth.

In socialist countries, the response was to turn economic power over to the state and let government planners decide what to produce and how to distribute it. In the capitalist world, Galbraith argued, similar power came to reside with large corporations. Companies would plan their production with only the crudest sense of what the consumer wanted. And then they would coax the consumer to buy with sophisticated advertising and marketing.

Consumers seemed to have little control over prices, as well. Most were fixed. The "manufacturer's suggested retail price" held sway. And in place of a market system, where clusters of merchants competed for the consumer's business on market day, goods were sold in retail outlets, with the nearest competition often miles away. Comparison-shopping was difficult and time-consuming.

Of course, consumers still had power in this system. If they chose not to buy a product—Ford's Edsel was the classic example— it would flop. If prices went too high, buyers could travel down the road to another store, or a competitor could come in and steal the business. But the textbook notion of consumer sovereignty often seemed more myth than reality.

Then came the revolution. Globalization meant that cozy oligopolies, like the big-three automakers—Ford, Chrysler, and General Motors—had to face scrappy, low-cost competitors, like Toyota, from overseas. Deregulation meant that the government rules that had been established to protect consumers but had come to protect entrenched producers were dismantled.

And most important, there was the digital revolution—the sudden ability of computers to transmit, store, and manipulate information over hundreds of miles, in hundreds of different directions, simultaneously. As a result, Adam Smith's atrophied network has gotten a dose of shock therapy. It has been revived, with a vengeance.

Galbraith's argument was that corporations had to plan the economy because lead times were so long and response times were so slow. But computer technology caused lead times and response times to evaporate. If consumers aren't buying a given product today, everyone in the corporation can find out, almost instantaneously, thanks to the computer network. And the production line can often be adjusted overnight, or instantaneously.

The consumer, meanwhile, faces more choices than ever. Giant discount chains compete with the corner retailer. Highly efficient national discount chains like Wal-Mart have squeezed the profit margins on almost everything. Competition is intense.

And then there is the Internet, which has expanded the consumer's horizons from his or her neighborhood to the world.

The Internet Advantage

Much has been made in recent years of the benefits of e-commerce. But actual buying over the Internet is still only a fraction of the nation's $5.8 trillion in consumer spending.

For now, the real value to the consumer of the Internet is not e-commerce, but information. By providing consumers with easy access to information, the Internet has already dramatically changed the relationship between consumers and sellers.

Think about buying a car. If you have ever gone to a car dealership without doing research, you know what an unpleasant experience that can be. A salesman will fill your ears with talk of rustproofing, financing plans, and options. He'll talk about how he is offering you a price so low that there's "barely any money left in this for the dealer." And you squirm in your chair. Why? Because the salesman has all the information, and you know only what he chooses to tell you.

Spend an hour on the Internet first, however, and the experience is completely different. You know in advance not just the sticker price, but the dealer's invoice. You know which options are worth buying and which aren't. You know exactly what car you want and how it compares with others in reliability and safety. And if you used an Internet buying service, you may even know the best price a dealer in the area is willing to give you.

Surveys suggest that roughly half of all car buyers now consult the web before buying. The same is happening in airline travel. The book-buying business has been transformed as well. And other businesses are following at a breakneck pace.

Recently, my nine-year-old daughter, Lucyann, decided we needed a digital camera, which would let us transfer photographs to our personal computer. If we had a digital camera, she explained, we could e-mail pictures to our friends.

Knowing little about digital cameras, I went to the Ritz Camera shop on the street level of the *Journal*'s Washington office building. The least expensive version there was a Kodak DC-210, with a zoom lens, for $499.

Then I went online, to a convenient service called Compare.net, now part of Microsoft's MSN.com e-shop, which gave me the basics on digital cameras. It told me, for instance, to pay attention to resolution, which is measured in pixels, and to memory, since that determines how many photos can be stored in the camera.

Following the site's simple instructions, I asked Compare.net to rank various digital cameras. The site showed that the manufacturer's suggested retail price for the Kodak DC-210 was $499—exactly what Ritz was charging. But it also had a "buy now" bug that took me to Buy.com, a retailer that claims to sell products on the web at or below cost. Buy.com was selling the DC-210 for $377—$122 below the Ritz price.

In about an hour's time, I had learned a lot about digital cameras, their differences, and their pricing. I decided $122 was too much to pay for the convenience of purchasing from a merchant in my building, and put off the purchase.

Three weeks later, I went back to Ritz and found they were having a sale—a "Ritz Blitz." The Kodak DC-210 was now on sale for $399—just $22 above the Buy.com price. The market was working.

"In economics classes, we used to talk about the frictions of information," says Sandra Shaber, a retail industry consultant. Consumers often paid higher prices than they needed to because they didn't have the time or energy or inclination to find out what the price should be. But a lot of that friction, says Shaber, has now disappeared. Finding the right price is easier than ever. And merchants know that if their price isn't right, competition is only a mouse click away.

The Internet is still in its infancy, and as it develops, the consumer's power is bound to increase in a variety of ways. In Adam Smith's market, consumers had only two choices: to buy or not to buy. But in the high-tech market, the consumer can send far more sophisticated messages.

Already, thousands of consumers are participating in auctions on sites like eBay.com and its competitors. And Priceline.com has turned the old economic model completely upside down, allowing consumers to set the price they are willing to pay while companies bid to serve them.

Moreover, the net allows consumers not only to say how much they'll pay for a product, but to design the product themselves.

Dell Computer has been at the forefront, but others are rapidly catching up.

I got a taste of that recently when my seven-year-old daughter, Amanda, received in the mail a CD-ROM called Dream Doll Designer. Conveniently, it arrived several weeks before her birthday. The program allowed her to design her own doll—down to the freckles and the brown bangs—and then order it. We fell for it; she loves the doll.

My shirtmaker at ShirtCreations.com is another example. A music shop called CDuctive Music (cductive.com) will let you mix songs from different artists and create your own CD, while Inter-Active Custom Clothes (ic3d.com) will let you tailor jeans to your figure.

All of this means that ever more control over the key decisions in the economy is now in the hands of consumers.

Business Fights Back

One of the great myths of American political culture is that businessmen love competition. They don't. Businessmen despise competition; it shifts power to the consumer.

The best in business—Bill Gates comes to mind—spend their waking hours plotting how to avoid competition and take the power of choice away from the consumer. Nothing frightens them more than the threat that their product or service is becoming a *commodity.* What economists call "perfect competition" is, for the businessperson, perfect hell.

So it's no surprise that, faced with an ever more competitive world, businesses are fighting back. They're looking for ways, as they have for decades, to escape from the harsh rigors of competition by differentiating their product, by creating popular brands, by advertising, by locking in their customers, or by trying anything else that increases their power to maintain higher prices than a competitive marketplace allows.

And in their struggle with the consumer, information technology provides them new tools as well. As information about individual consumers becomes more available, businesses are learning to become more sophisticated at using it to discriminate among buyers. Rather than have one price for their product, they have multiple prices, designed to get each consumer to pay the maximum he or she is willing to pay. If you are a bargain shopper, they'll give you a good price; but if you aren't inclined to shop around and you have a taste for extravagance, prepare to be fleeced.

The airlines have become masters at this game, often offering more different fares than there are seats on a plane. Software companies are also becoming skilled discriminators, appealing to the bargain shopper with a low-priced "standard" version and to the status-conscious with a high-priced "deluxe."

Amazon.com is leading the way to the next level of marketing sophistication. When you buy a book at Amazon, the company offers you three or four others that it has picked, based on its knowledge of your interests. Increasingly, a visit to Amazon is like walking into a bookstore that's been designed with your particular interests in mind. You like cooking? Well, the cooking section is right inside the front door. You have young children? The latest Harry Potter book is waiting at the checkout counter. And as Amazon expands into toys and electronic products, its ability to cross-market those products will grow rapidly.

My friend Robert Rosiello, a senior partner at McKinsey and Company, likes to say that the most profitable words in the English language are uttered by McDonald's clerks, who ask "Would you like French fries with that?" Businesses have found that a simple suggestion, made at the right moment, can prompt a sale of a high-margin product that otherwise might not have happened.

Technology will eventually allow companies to know your particular tastes and to offer you the equivalent of French fries, tailored to those tastes, with each product or service you purchase.

The point is this: In the New Economy, consumers hold the power. But profit-hungry companies with ever more information about you are going to get ever better at coaxing, luring, pushing, and urging you to exercise that power in a way that will boost their profits.

This isn't all bad. Some of the personalized marketing may prove valuable to you. If you like mystery novels, Amazon will make sure you know when a hot new one comes out. If your credit card records show you eat frequently at Chinese restaurants, you may get discount coupons when a new one opens in town.

But much of this marketing will also be designed to take advantage of you, perhaps at a moment of confusion or weakness. After all, it's no secret that McDonald's sells French fries; if you had really wanted them, you could have ordered them in the first place.

Eight Tips to Surviving and Thriving as a Consumer in the New Economy

So how can you make the most of your new power as a consumer? The main point to remember is that you are in control. Businesses have to respond to your needs because you have choices. If they don't, you'll go elsewhere, and they will lose business.

But keep in mind also that the business world is getting better than ever at pushing your hot buttons. Businesses have countless schemes for getting you to part with money when you probably shouldn't. You've got the power; but you've got to exercise it wisely.

The following tips are for making your way as a consumer in the New Economy. Follow them closely, and they'll pay dividends.

1. Don't pay the sticker price

The days of fixed prices are over. It doesn't matter whether you are buying a house, a car, or a video camera; in the New Economy, the smart consumer needn't pay full price. Ask local merchants to match prices you've seen on the Internet. Ask if coupons are available. Ask when the next sale is going to be held.

Remember: The key to business survival in the New Economy is to make you pay as much as you are willing. If you don't look for bargains, if you don't ask for a better price, then you'll pay through the nose. But if you push a little, you'll be amazed how often prices will fall.

2. Don't buy on impulse

The information highway is a two-way street. You can find out more than ever before about the products and services you want to buy and the companies that are selling them. But those companies can also find out more about you. And as they learn, don't be surprised to find them appealing to your basest instincts. Have a weakness for chocolate? The day may come when Amazon.com offers you a box while you browse for books. Resist. Take a few deep breaths. And if you decide you really want chocolate, comparison-shop.

3. "Just say no" to the extras

Rustproofing on your car, service contracts on electrical appliances, pre-paid gasoline in your rental car—these are all gimmicks devised by businesses to make you shell out more money at the cash register. They are offered to you at the last minute, and you are urged by a salesperson to say yes.

Invariably, these last-minute add-ons are high-profit items for the business, which means they probably aren't a good deal for you. So practice saying no to retail clerks. It's almost always the right answer. Buy what you want, not what they want you to. You have the power; don't give it away.

4. Don't pay for something you can get for free

In the textbook market economy, competition drives prices down to the marginal cost—the cost of producing one more item. But in the information world, the marginal cost is often zero. As a result, competitive pressure can push prices to the disappearing point—as happened when Microsoft and Netscape were competing to win the market for computer web browsers.

You'll be amazed at the free products and services available on the Internet: free software, free newspapers, free music, free faxes, free greeting cards, free Internet hookups, free phone calls. Before you pay money for a service—Internet access, for instance—check around to see if you can get what you need at no cost.

5. Don't buy the silver or gold version when brass will do

In the New Economy, companies are constantly trying to divide their customers between those who insist on the lowest price and those who are willing to pay a little, or a lot, extra. One way they do that is by offering different versions of their service or product, in hopes that you'll agree to pay more. Don't be taken in by words like "deluxe" and "professional"; if the standard package has everything you need, buy it.

6. Don't assume that if you buy something on the Internet, you're getting a good price

You may not be. Because comparison-shopping is so easy on the web, many analysts thought competition would automatically drive down all web prices. But studies show that has not happened. In fact, one MIT study found that prices actually vary more in cyberspace than they do in the physical world. The price for a single book, for instance, can differ by as much as 47 percent across Internet retailers at any time, even though it's relatively easy to search the Internet for the lowest price.

So shop around. Comparison-shopping is easy on the web. If it's a book you're after, for instance, you can go to isbn.nu, type in the book's ISBN (the identifying number on the copyright page), and get an instant price comparison of major online booksellers.

7. Be flexible

Businesses make their money off your intransigence. If you are a creature of habit, if you insist on buying a certain brand, or if you are simply too busy or hassled to bother with comparison-shopping, you will always pay more. Indeed, in the New Economy, where consumers face more demands on their time and attention than ever before, the greatest asset a company can have is an installed, loyal base of customers. That's because those customers would usually rather pay more than switch.

Consider this: It's been a decade and a half since the breakup of AT&T, and most consumers have never changed their phone service.

You'll do better if you do switch occasionally. It's a way of making clear that you're going to insist on the best product at the lowest price.

8. But don't switch without getting something in return

Businesses today know their biggest challenge is building a loyal customer base, and they set aside huge portions of their budgets to do so. They know that consumers are reluctant to switch away from a trusted brand or service, and so they are prepared to pay heavily to get you to switch. That's why phone companies are forever sending you $50 checks and other freebies to get you to sign on to their service, or why credit card companies offer 3.9 percent introductory rates.

One of my friends says the cheapest and easiest strategy for managing your long-distance phone service is to switch servers each time you get a new offer. If that strikes you as more trouble than it's worth, try this: Go to Inc.com, which will help you figure out which long-distance service is best for you, given your pattern of calling. Then call a customer service representative at that company and ask whether they have any special incentives they give new customers. Odds are, they will.

BUYING ON THE WEB

The Internet world is changing so rapidly that it's difficult to provide guidance in a book. Today's hot website may be gone tomorrow, and another one will have sprung up to take its place.

Moreover, keeping up with the constant outpouring of new e-commerce websites is more than anyone can manage. Some are highly specialized: Discounturns.com, for instance, sells nothing but an array of urns to hold the remains of your cremated loved ones. Others are hopelessly general: A hotly promoted new site called Shopnow.com is little more than a directory of all the other online stores. Because it makes its money from the stores that list with it, it doesn't provide any tools to help you compare prices.

Here's a review of some of the sites my associate Keith Perine found useful when facing life's big purchasing decisions.

Automobiles Three websites lead the way in helping you to narrow your choice of cars, decide on options, and learn what the right price should be. They are Edmund's (edmunds.com), IntelliChoice.com, and Kelley Blue Book

---

(kbb.com). These sites will help you comparison-shop and narrow down your options according to price range and style. You can also check on Consumer Reports Online (consumerreports.org).

After you've chosen the car you want, there are several ways to use the Internet to ease your purchase. Autobytel.com is the largest service, selling $500 million in cars a month in 1999. The company will refer you to a traditional dealer who will then quote a favorable price; or, in a newer service, it will let you "click and buy" a car immediately at a fixed price. There's a hybrid of services that refer you to dealers—such as Microsoft's CarPoint.com and Autoweb.com—as well as those that deliver you a car directly— such as CarsDirect.com. It's worth noting, though, that even CarsDirect.com gets its cars through a dealer.

To test the convenience of buying a new car online, Keith asked several of the websites to research a new Ford Explorer sport utility vehicle. A quick trip to the National Highway Traffic Safety Administration's website (nhtsa.dot.gov) confirmed that no recalls or service bulletins had been issued for new Explorers. The autovantage.com site of America Online Inc. provided a four-page report on the Explorer that rated such factors as acceleration, fuel economy, and handling.

Satisfied with the choice, he submitted a purchase request on Autobytel.com that specified model, color, transmission type, and options. A salesperson at Ourisman Ford in nearby Alexandria, Virginia, called later the same day with a "no hassle, no haggle" price of $30,489—just $100 over the dealer invoice and more than $3,000 less than the sticker price.

Travel Travel is another area where the Internet has already transformed the business. Like car salesmen, travel agents often pay more attention to their commissions than to your best interests. But the Internet gives you access to the same information they have and allows you to choose the best deal.

To test how well this worked, Keith planned a vacation for two to Costa Rica through Travelocity.com and Expedia .com and compared the costs with quotes from Washington-area travel agents.

Travelocity's site sent him to the Online Vacation Mall, where he priced a package including round-trip airfare from Washington, D.C., to San Jose, Costa Rica's capital city, and five nights' stay in a mid-range hotel. The cost: $1,432, before taxes, transfers, and insurance. For $75, a whitewater rafting trip could be added to the itinerary.

On Expedia's website, airline tickets and hotel reservations came to a similar cost: $1,535.

Local travel agents were hard-pressed to duplicate the seamless experience offered by the online sites. Keith called Van Ness Travel in Washington and was put on hold for four minutes, then told to call back in two weeks, after the "vacation travel agent" returned to the office. After a couple of days and a few exchanged phone messages, two other local travel agencies—Destinations and Circle Travel Inc.—priced the Costa Rica getaway at $1,718 and $1,535, respectively. The Destinations agent said that subsequent pricing requests would cost $50 because, as the agent put it, "nobody likes to work for free."

Mortgages and Other Credit Consumers who want to shop for a mortgage online can now go straight to sites like bankrate.com, theloanpage.com, and lendingtree.com. The sites offer mortgage rate quotes, definitions of terms such as "ARM" and "amortization," and answers to questions that borrowers frequently ask.

For life insurance, try insurancepage.com, where you can get life insurance rate quotes, based on your age, sex, height, and weight, from dozens of companies. Intuit's Quicken InsureMarket.com site provides a comprehensive directory of real-time quotes, insurance information, agent contacts, and policies offered by leading American insurance companies.

Long-Distance Phone Service The breakup of AT&T and the deregulation of phone service represents both the best and the worst of the New Economy. It's the best because it has led to a deluge of fierce competition, sharply reducing the cost of calling. But it's the worst because of its complexity; in their efforts to divide up the market, phone companies have devised amazingly intricate pricing schemes that can baffle a mathematics whiz. Unless you want to spend your leisure time reading fine print on those direct mail offers, there seemed to be no good answer.

But now there is. Two websites offer powerful tools that will help you sort through the jumble and find the right plan.

Before you start, get your hands on a typical monthly bill. Plan prices vary depending on when you make your calls—morning, evening, night—and also where you call. At Inc.com, you can enter a month's worth of phone calls and have the program analyze your habits and suggest the best service, or you can summarize your own calling habits and get the same thing. Another useful site is TRAC WebPricer (trac.org/webpricer/).

You'll be surprised at what a big difference the right plan makes. On one 25-minute call we made, for instance, the price varied from $4.49 on MCI's basic service to $1.25 on a QWest plan.

5

Health Care in the New Economy

Your Choice, Your Responsibility

Nothing has changed more dramatically—more *traumatically*—in the New Economy than the relationship between you and your doctor.

A generation ago, that relationship was one of trust. If you were sick, you went to the family doctor. If you needed hospitalization, your doctor put you in the hospital where he or she practiced. There was no *marketplace* for health care, because to have a marketplace you have to have consumers who can make choices based on available information. Health care patients weren't true consumers; they had few choices and little information. Cost wasn't an issue because, most of the time, someone else was paying the bill.

Today, that's changed. A revolution has occurred in health care. Businesses rebelled against soaring health insurance costs in the 1980s and early 1990s and demanded managed care—injecting themselves into the relationship between doctor and patient. People lost faith in their doctors and hospitals—just as they lost faith in other powerful institutions in society—and began to ask questions and demand choices. Doctors became "health care providers"; patients became "clients." The world of health care, insulated for most of the twentieth century from the manipulations of Adam Smith's invisible hand, suddenly became a marketplace, with a bewildering array of options and choices.

It's a frightening marketplace. After all, undergoing a coronary bypass operation is a lot different from buying a car. Choices are nice, but the *responsibility* that goes with choice in health care can be awesome. In the old days, for better or worse, you trusted your doctor to do what was right. Today, you must trust yourself. Have you chosen the right doctor? The right hospital? Are you sure you are getting the right advice, the right treatment? Is your insurance company or health care service elevating concerns about cost over concerns about your health? These questions are all the more difficult because they are so often accompanied by powerful emotions. Markets work when people make rational decisions; but how can you be rational when your life or the life of a loved one is involved?

It's also a badly flawed marketplace. Doctors and hospitals still cling to the old ways and resist relinquishing their monopoly over medical information. Getting good information about the quality of a doctor's or a hospital's care is difficult or impossible. And without good information about quality, the marketplace can't work.

My father's illness helped educate me to the problems in the health care marketplace. In early 1997, he had been in the hospital for major surgery—the early days of his battle with cancer. He was recovering and was about to be discharged. Then one Friday afternoon I got a call from my brother, Lee. Things weren't going well, he said; I'd better come to Chattanooga right away.

When I arrived that evening, I found my father on death's edge, but not because of cancer. He had acquired what's called a hospital infection—an infection resistant to antibiotics. It had ripped through his body, and he was in a state of septic shock—unconscious, quivering, kept alive only with huge doses of powerful drugs that constricted his blood vessels and forced up his blood pressure from what otherwise would have been deadly low levels.

He stayed in that state for more than forty-eight hours, his doctors and nurses warning us that he could die at any time. Then, miraculously, he began to recover. His blood pressure rose, the medicine dosage was decreased, and consciousness slowly, fitfully, returned.

By Monday, he could see us and hear us, but he couldn't talk because of the tubes down his throat. So we got a board with the letters of the alphabet, and we spelled out words by pointing to each letter and getting him to nod his head if it was the one he wanted. Slowly, through this painstaking process, he communicated his first message:

"Get a lawyer."

My father got over his urge to sue. But his request led me to do some research. I learned that ninety thousand people a year die from hospital infections and that many of those deaths probably could have been prevented with cleanliness: a sterile operating room, a clean hospital, and most important, clean hands.

The more I learned, the more I wondered: Had Erlanger Hospital been the best place for my father's care? Did it follow the very best procedures in avoiding infections? There were other hospitals in Chattanooga and scores of hospitals in nearby Nashville and Atlanta. Should he have shopped around?

I tried to find out whether Erlanger had an unusually high rate of hospital infections, but quickly learned that that information isn't available. I logged on to the website of the Joint Commission on Accreditation of Healthcare Organizations (jcaho.org), where I was told Erlanger had recently been accredited "with recommendations for improvement." What did that mean? A note further down told me it meant the hospital "does not meet certain important standards in one area." What was that one area? I clicked on an icon that promised a full performance report, only to get a message that said the performance report was "not available at this time." Nor were "performance reports" available for any of the other hospitals I checked.

A little further research let me know that I wasn't alone in my frustration. A woman named Karen Burton had sued the University of Iowa a few years earlier for refusing to disclose its hospital's infection rate. A district court ruled in her favor, but the state supreme court overturned the ruling.

Hospital administrators argue passionately against revealing such information to the public. For one thing, they say, the data might give a distorted picture; after all, not all hospital infections are preventable by the hospital, and many come, as one put it, "from the patient's own bacteria." For another, big hospitals that take care of really sick patients might show "unfairly" high infection rates, compared to smaller, suburban hospitals. The government's Centers for Disease Control collects voluntary data and monitors individual hospital infection rates, but won't make the data public. A CDC official argues that if such information were made public, hospitals might "game the system" and deliberately underreport their infection rates.

I found all this frustrating. If, in the New Economy, I have to take responsibility for health care choices, then shouldn't I also have access to relevant information? Didn't my father have a right to know whether the hospital he was choosing was clean? In a truly efficient market, hospitals might feel pressure to do what some fast-food restaurants have started doing: require employees to wear bracelets with computer chips on their arms that document frequent hand washing. Isn't the cleanliness of a hospital attendant at least as important as that of a fast-food cook?

Without good data on quality, the new market for health care can have perverse effects. Hospitals, for instance, have come under heavy pressure to cut costs in recent years. One way they do that is by reducing their nursing staff. But in some cases, studies after the fact have shown that a reduction in nursing staffs has raised the infection rate. For the market to work, hospitals need to show they are maintaining quality at the same time they are reducing cost.

A few states—Pennsylvania and New York in particular—have led the way in insisting that consumers be provided detailed information about the performance of hospitals and doctors in their states. In Pennsylvania, the state legislature created the Pennsylvania Health Care Cost Containment Council in 1986. The independent state agency collects more than two million inpatient hospital discharge records every year. The council uses its database to publish analyses of the cost and quality of health care in the state.

While its ostensible purpose is to help health care purchasers keep down costs, the council simultaneously performs a valuable public service for Pennsylvania state residents. The council has published eighty reports on the treatment of conditions ranging

THE WEALTH OF CHOICES

from asthma to gunshot wounds, which are available online (phc4.org) and in most public libraries across the state.

And the availability of the data has made a difference. My *Journal* colleague Ron Winslow wrote a fascinating story about Lehigh Valley Hospital, which protested loudly the first time its highly regarded heart program got a poor grade in 1992—and then went to work to improve the program. "It got the doctors' attention," said Robert Laskowski, chief medical officer at the hospital.

In New York, data on risk-adjusted mortality rates for heart bypass surgery, broken out by hospital and individual surgeons, has been published since 1989. Physicians and hospitals were initially opposed to publication of the data, arguing that the statistics were too subjective to be relied upon. But the health department persisted, and the statewide mortality rate for such surgery fell sharply in the first four years after the data were published. Once they knew they were going to be held accountable, doctors and hospitals did a better job.

These are the exceptions, not the rule. Doctors and hospitals are still resisting the inevitable move into the New Economy. If you visit the website of the American Medical Association (ama-assn.org), for instance, you can look up the names of your doctors, but you won't learn a lot. You can find out where they went to medical school and whether they are board certified and how to get to their office—but not much else.

But that will change, and is changing. Under market pressure from managed care companies, the AMA has already created a new evaluation system, which will be in place nationwide by 2004. To be accredited, doctors will have to be free of disciplinary actions, have

108

completed at least a hundred hours of continuing education, and undergo an office site review. Accreditations will occur every two years.

And hospital information is beginning to become more widely available as well. At a website called HealthGrades.com, more than five thousand hospitals are graded on a one-star to five-star scale for their performance in certain operations. I learned, for instance, that Chattanooga's Erlanger Hospital received only three stars for coronary bypass surgery, based on mortality rates among its patients, while nearby Memorial Hospital had five stars.

Such data are fraught with complications. Hospitals who treat the sickest patients, for instance, will naturally have the highest mortality rates; thus the statistics have to be adjusted for "risk"—a tricky statistical procedure. And the size of the hospital can distort the numbers too. If one hospital performs fifty bypasses a year with forty-five of them successful, while a second hospital performs only ten, but all of them successful, who really has the better record? The second hospital has the better batting average, but the first clearly has more experience. HealthGrades.com deals with that problem by putting "low volume" hospitals into a separate category.

Unfortunately, health care providers aren't the only ones slow to make the transition to the New Economy. Many health care consumers are too. Michael Millenson, author of an excellent book, *Demanding Medical Excellence,* notes that the vast majority of coronary bypass patients in Pennsylvania weren't even aware of the state's excellent guide to doctors and hospitals that conduct such operations. And of those who were aware, few said the guide influenced their choice of a doctor or hospital.

That's a shame. In the New Economy, the consumer has a right to good information. But he or she also has an obligation to make wise use of that information.

Information Empowerment

While good information about doctors, hospitals, and health plans is still hard to come by, good information about diseases and treatments isn't. The last decade has seen an explosion in publicly available health care information. And as a result, the relationship between doctor and patient has been transformed. Patients now come armed with information and are often intelligent participants in their own care.

In the old economy, patients had, as Oliver Wendell Holmes once put it, "no more right to all the truth than . . . to all the medicine in your saddlebags." In the New Economy, health care has become a two-way street.

Dr. David Nash, of Thomas Jefferson University, calls this "information empowerment," going from being passive participants in our own health care to being "self-care" consumers, independently seeking the information we need to help manage our care. Says Millenson: "Now, when a doctor says to a woman 'You need a mastectomy,' she might understand there are options."

When forty-three-year-old Susan Gordon was facing a hysterectomy, she researched the pros and cons of epidural and general anesthesia. By visiting hysterectomy patient chat rooms, such as HysterSisters (hystersisters.org), she found out that general anesthesia would leave her feeling groggy until the drug wore off completely. By contrast, an epidural would simply numb the relevant nerve endings, leaving Gordon free to get back to work soon after her surgery. Gordon says her anesthesiologist was surprised that she'd done her homework, but readily agreed to use an epidural during Gordon's surgery.

New sources of information appear on the Internet almost every day. When thirty-one-year-old Art Flatau was diagnosed with leukemia in 1992, he used a family medical guide, a Peanuts video-tape from the Leukemia Society of America, and a research article given to him by his doctor to help himself and his family under-stand his condition. Today, Flatau, in partnership with another leukemia survivor, Barbara Lackritz, runs GrannyBarb and Art's Leukemia Links (acor.org/leukemia), a web page that doubles as a support system and information clearinghouse for leukemia pa-tients. Dozens of links to research articles and abstracts, mailing lists, news and chat groups, and other survivors' stories are com-bined to offer patients hundreds of pages of information, ranging from how to live with leukemia to the latest clinical trials.

"There was hardly anything online before," Flatau says. "There was a news group with one woman who'd had a bone marrow transplant—now we have an eight-hundred-person mailing list."

For one family facing a catastrophic illness, the massive amount of publicly available data played a key role in shaping treatment decisions.

When twenty-eight-year-old Brian Zikmund-Fisher was first diagnosed with myelodysplastic syndrome (MDS), a progressive bone marrow disorder, in March 1998, he and his wife, Naomi, were mainly relieved that it wasn't leukemia. But when Naomi logged on to the Internet and searched "myelodysplastic syndrome" on Yahoo.com, she found research journal articles that predicted a life expectancy of five years or less.

"I started reading, and my eyes got bigger and bigger," Naomi says.

After Naomi's initial testing of the waters, the Zikmund-Fishers, self-described medical research junkies, plunged into the Internet to find out all they could about the disease. Naomi soon discovered that the short life expectancy predictions were largely owed to the fact that most MDS patients were more than sixty years old. Brian's age worked in his favor, but it also made him a rare case.

Naomi found articles that recommended bone marrow transplants, and Brian's doctor soon agreed that he needed to undergo a transplant within the next year. When the doctor prescribed Danazol, a growth hormone, to check the deterioration of Brian's blood platelets, Naomi went back to Yahoo. She discovered that only one in three MDS patients responded to the drug and that possible side effects included liver problems and hair loss. Fortunately, Brian responded well to the drug.

Brian initially hoped to have a transplant performed at the Western Pennsylvania Cancer Institute. The institute's doctors enthusiastically recommended a transplant with T-cell depletion, in which T-cells are removed from the donated marrow prior to the transplant. Ostensibly, that would decrease the chances that Brian's immune system would destroy the transplanted bone marrow.

But when Naomi posted a question about T-cell-depleted transplants on BMT Talk (BMTsupport.org), an online bone marrow transplant support group, she was e-mailed by a doctor in Minnesota who told her that the procedure was still experimental and actually carried a greater chance of graft failure.

The specialist at West Penn who had championed T-cell-depleted transplants backpedaled in the face of the new information, so the Zikmund-Fishers decided to shop around for another hospital. The National Marrow Donor Program at Boston's Dana-Farber Cancer Institute (dfci.harvard.edu) provided a directory of bone marrow transplant centers, along with statistics on their track records. The directory showed that the Fred Hutchinson Cancer Research Center, located in Seattle, had the best statistics. They performed a relatively high number of MDS transplants annually, and their survival rate was good. Brian underwent a bone marrow transplant in May 1998.

No amount of data can adequately prepare you for the serious illness of a loved one. The best you can hope for is that your spade-work will help you make sense of events and that you'll be able to guide your decisions with the latest research available.

Washington Post reporter Marc Fisher dove into what he calls "the roiling sea of information that is medicine today" when his nineteen-month-old son was diagnosed with an Arnold Chiari (key-AR-ee) malformation in early 1998. As Fisher and his wife climbed the physician ladder from pediatrician to internist to specialist, the reporter searched musty medical libraries, online support groups, and MedLine for data on the rare congenital condition in which extra brain tissue extends into the spinal cord. Without treatment, Fisher's son faced neurological disorders and paralysis.

Fisher's online research led him to Georgetown University's medical library, where he researched the old-fashioned way—by poring through a stack of thick medical journals.

When Fisher discussed his findings with the specialists, reactions were mixed. Some doctors encouraged him to find out all he could and share it with them. Others warned Fisher not to pin his hopes on unsubstantiated recommendations he unearthed on the web.

Because of his experiences, Fisher advises patients to probe their doctors carefully and to avoid physicians who refuse to discuss independent research. "If they don't want to discuss what you're reading and finding, then flee," says Fisher.

But Fisher cautions that the tips and advice that can be found in online chat rooms, which he describes as "a product of people typing in spare bedrooms at 2:00 A.M. thousands of miles away," should be taken with a grain of salt. "You get everything from the most pathetic sob stories to useful information, and it's hard to know which is which," Fisher says.

Although Arnold Chiari malformations had been an acknowledged medical condition for decades, most of the surgical strategies were new enough that Fisher was unable to find long-term or multi-hospital studies to reassure himself and his wife about the best course of action.

After reading online medical articles; consulting with doctors across the country via e-mail, telephone, and personal visits; and searching LEXIS-NEXIS, the Fishers asked Robert Keating, a pediatric surgeon at Children's Hospital in Washington, D.C., to perform neurosurgery on their son. Keating's operation loosened the passageway from their son's spinal cord to his brain, allowing fluid to get past the obstructing tissue.

Today, Fisher's son's condition is managed with prescription drugs, the possible side effects of which Fisher carefully researched online, at sites such as MedLine.com and OnHealth.com.

Good Information and Bad Information

As Fisher's experience illustrates, information is plentiful in the New Economy. But *good* information is less so. And distinguishing between good and bad information is getting ever more difficult.

Websites can be put up and taken down faster than a snake oil salesman's clapboard wagon. And some of them are offering advice that's no more sound.

The National Vaccine Information Center (909shot.com) is an example. It looks and sounds like it might be a government-sponsored clearinghouse for vaccine information. In fact, according to my friend Dr. Bruce Gellin, an infectious disease specialist, it was set up by two women whose children had adverse reactions to the first generation DPT vaccine (diphtheria-pertussis-tetanus) in the 1970s. The group claims it isn't opposed to vaccines, but the site is jammed with heart-wrenching anecdotes of children harmed by vaccines and an array of materials that oppose childhood vaccinations. The site never makes clear that the established medical consensus is that the risks of most childhood vaccines are quite small compared to the benefits. The site's logo graphic is a hypodermic needle that could skewer an automobile engine block.

The web is filled with similar sources of both misinformation (information that is incomplete and out of date) and disinformation (information that is put out with a deliberate disregard for prevailing medical opinion).

Medical chat rooms, in particular, can turn out to be purveyors of bad advice. For people suffering from rare diseases, the websites can provide a much-needed link to others suffering from the same condition. But often, these chat rooms are frequented by *cyberchon-*

driacs, who seem to wallow in their illness. And the value of the information that's conveyed on the site is anyone's guess.

To avoid disinformation and misinformation, it's best to look for sites with established reputations or sites linked to well-regarded institutions or government agencies. The website Drkoop-.com, for instance, trades on the reputation of former Surgeon General C. Everett Koop—although that reputation has been tarnished a bit by some early missteps in the launching of the company and by reports he was receiving payments from advertisers on the site. Another popular site, Intellihealth.com, promises information that's been vetted by the medical experts at Johns Hopkins University. And the Seattle-based OnHealth Network (onhealth.com) pulls information from respected sources like the New England Journal of Medicine and Harvard University.

In addition, there are numerous academic sites, like the cancer patients' site at the University of Pennsylvania Medical Center (oncolink.upenn.edu). And there are a wealth of government sites, such as the one run by the Centers for Disease Control (cdc.com), the National Institutes of Health's National Library of Medicine (nlm.nih.gov), or the healthfinder.gov site maintained by the U.S. Department of Health and Human Services.

For better or worse, advertising is also becoming a significant source of information on health care. A generation ago, companies that made prescription drugs or medical equipment would market directly to doctors, because the doctors had all the power. But today they have started marketing directly to consumers, because consumers now make the choices. And the early signs are that the impact of that change has been powerful.

In 1997, the Food and Drug Administration eased its guidelines

allowing drug companies to advertise prescription drugs to consumers. The following year, drug companies spent $8.3 billion pro-
moting their products, including $1.3 billion advertising directly
to consumers, according to a study by the National Institute for
Health Care Management. Among the most heavily advertised
drugs were the antihistamines Claritin, Zyrtech, and Allegra, which
were promoted with $313 million worth of consumer advertising.
Sales for those antihistamines soared.

Indeed, one study found that doctor visits for heavily advertised
conditions rose 11 percent between January and September of that
year. Another survey found that 53 percent of physicians reported
an increase in requests for drugs by brand name, up from just 30
percent in 1997. Consumers were going to the doctor and demanding a prescription drug they had heard advertised, and the doctors
were complying.

"It's a double-edged sword," says Nancy Chockley, who heads
the National Institute for Health Care Management. "These advertisements help raise people's awareness about certain illnesses, like
sexual dysfunction," she says, referring to former presidential aspi-
rant Bob Dole's Viagra advertisements. "But there's a danger in people getting too far out in front of their doctors, and going in and
demanding the medication. Many doctors decide it's easier to write
the prescription; why argue the patient doesn't really need it?"

Seven Questions to Ask When Facing a Major Medical Procedure

Most of us don't know how to be good health care consumers. Our
parents put their faith in the family doctor; they never learned, and
never taught us, how to shop for care. But often, health care choices

are the most important we'll make in life. When faced with the prospect of a major medical problem or procedure, ask yourself the following seven questions.

1. Have I done my homework?

In the New Economy, your health care is your responsibility, as well as your doctor's. You ought to spend more time researching a major surgery or procedure than you would researching a new car.

2. Do I really need this procedure or treatment?

Many health care experts believe the health care system in this country often overprescribes surgery and other invasive and risky procedures. In a presentation at a conference sponsored by the National Institute for Health Care Management, Dr. Mark Chassin cited cardiac pacemakers, hysterectomies, and coronary angiographies as three examples of common health services that are used more often than they should be. In health care, supply often seems to create its own demand. If an area has lots of hospital beds per capita, for instance, people tend to spend more time in the hospital. If it has lots of eye specialists, eye operations may be more common.

Get a second opinion.

3. Is this procedure or treatment a standard practice nationwide?

To a frightening degree, geography is destiny in American health care. A man's odds of having his prostate removed, for instance, can be ten times higher in some parts of the country than others. That's not because rates of prostate cancer are higher, but because of wide variations in the prescribed treatment—doctors in many areas will prescribe "watchful waiting" for older men who are likely to die before the disease takes hold. In other areas, they operate. The same goes for many diagnostic procedures; female Medicare patients in Traverse City, Michigan, for instance, are four times as likely to receive a mammogram to detect early-stage breast cancer as their counterparts in El Paso, Texas.

4. Does the doctor I've chosen do this operation or procedure often? Does the hospital do the operation or procedure often?

Go with experience. In a world where information on the quality of doctors and hospitals is hard to come by, experience is the best proxy. Studies have shown that the surgeons and the hospitals that do the most coronary bypass operations tend to have the lowest mortality rates. The same is true with many other operations.

5. Is my doctor certified?

The AMA board certification process (ama-assn.org) doesn't provide you much information; but if a doctor *hasn't* gotten his certification, you'd better take it seriously.

6. Is the hospital accredited?

The same goes here. The Joint Commission on Accreditation of Health Organizations (jcaho.org) gives you unnervingly little detail, but it does scour hospital data pretty thoroughly. If yours doesn't get an unqualified accreditation, you might want to look elsewhere.

7. Is my doctor or specialist willing to freely discuss information I've found on the web?

Sure, the doctor went through years of education to get where he or she is. And no amount of web research can replace the wisdom of a skilled physician. But you have a right—a *responsibility*—to participate in the determination of your own health care. "You don't tell the pilot how to fly the plane," says Michael Millenson. But you can, and should, "have a strong opinion about where you're going."

You also get to choose the pilot. If your doctor is uncomfortable discussing information you've uncovered, find another doctor.

CHOOSING A HEALTH CARE PLAN

Many working Americans now have a choice of health care plans. But choosing among plans, particularly when you're still healthy, can be a challenge.

The National Committee on Quality Assurance (ncqa. org) rates health plans on various standards and can provide a useful reference. But interpreting NCQA's data can be a struggle. A survey by *U.S. News and World Report,* for instance, used NCQA's data and gave Kaiser of Northern California its lowest grade of 1. But *Newsweek* magazine scoured the same data and gave Kaiser of Northern California its highest rating of 4.

Another organization that attempts to rank health plans is The American Accreditation Healthcare Commission/ URAC, located on the web at urac.org. But its data can be equally difficult to interpret.

Nancy Chockley of NIHCM recommends you choose a health care plan based on your particular needs. If you have young children, make sure the pediatric care is good. If one of those children has asthma, make sure there's a first-rate asthma program linked in. Also look carefully to see what's included; are prescription drugs, dental work, or eyeglasses part of the package?

In addition, here are five questions to ask when evaluating a health plan.

1. Does the plan offer preventive services, such as mammograms and cholesterol screenings?

2. How easy is it to see a specialist under the plan?

3. Are people already in the plan happy with their coverage and the service they receive?

4. How does the plan select physicians? Does my doctor participate?

5. Does the plan cover preexisting conditions? How does it treat ongoing or chronic conditions?

6

Education in the New Economy

Your Mind Is Your Best Investment

Throughout the twentieth century, futurists have worried that technology would dehumanize society. Books like *Brave New World* and *1984* depict a future in which human creativity and originality are stifled in the name of order and control. François Truffaut's film *Fahenheit 451*, based on the book by Ray Bradbury, is a classic of the genre, depicting a society that burned all books in order to avoid seditious thoughts.

But as a new millennium begins, it's clear that the New Economy values nothing more than a creative, well-educated mind. Machines and computers can do many of the tasks once done by human beings; but they can't replicate the human imagination. As a result, an imaginative, educated human mind has become the most valued asset.

A few simple figures make the point. In 1980, an American with a college degree earned $4,666 more, on average, than one without—a 42 percent difference. By 1997, that difference had risen to

$14,745, or 74 percent. Women with college degrees earn, on average, *double* what women without degrees earn.

Multiply those higher earnings over a lifetime, and you'll see that it's indisputable: An education is the best investment you can make. And it's a good investment not just because it teaches you particular skills—odds are any skills you learn in college will quickly become as obsolete as the slide rule. Rather, education is a good investment because it trains you to think, and thinking is your ticket to the New Economy.

But there's a catch: While the market forces of today's economy have raised the value of education, they've been slow to infiltrate the processes of education. "Efficiency" and "productivity" may be watchwords in most modern institutions, but they still raise eyebrows in the faculty lounge. College professors are still swathed in lifetime tenure. And college tuition continues to rise far faster than inflation and remains seemingly impervious to competition.

For many middle-income families, that poses a conundrum. The value of a first-class college education has never been higher; but neither has the cost. It pays to get yourself or your children the best education available. But the cost of that education may be more than you can bear.

This chapter will look at how the New Economy is slowly finding its way inside the ivy-covered walls of America's most prestigious universities, which occupy the top of the higher-education pyramid. Then it will take a look at the revolution that's happening at the bottom of that pyramid, as creative distance-learning programs rapidly expand their influence. Eventually, the pressures at the top and bottom are bound to transform higher education, making it more flexible, more efficient, and more affordable—just as the pressures of the New Economy have transformed every other business.

Finally, this chapter will look at some recent innovations in financing higher education. In today's world, you can't afford anything less than the best education available; these financing techniques will help you do it.

Haggling with Harvard

Look at how rapidly tuitions are rising at the nation's top colleges and universities, and you might conclude these institutions are sheltered from the powerful winds of change that have swept the rest of the economy. But look more closely, and you'll see that change is occurring.

For one thing, despite steady tuition increases, prices have come unglued. For a growing number of families, college tuitions today are no more meaningful than the sticker price on an automobile. College administrators don't like to admit this; they still talk euphemistically of fixed tuitions and financial aid packages that vary strictly according to need. But in the last few years, even many of the most elite schools have thrown in the towel. "Discounting" is rampant. "When April comes," says one person familiar with the practices at top-tier schools, "increasingly, it's 'Let's make a deal.' "

Yes, you can even haggle at Harvard. Joyce Keck of Laredo, Texas, was one of the first to learn that lesson, in 1998. A class valedictorian with an SAT score of 1510 (out of 1600), Joyce was accepted by Harvard, but received a more generous financial aid offer from Rice University in Houston. Her parents, a nurse and a college professor, made comfortable salaries. But the $30,000-a-year cost of sending Joyce to Harvard seemed out of reach, even with the aid the school offered.

So Joyce's mother, Patricia Keck, sent a fax to Harvard explaining her quandary, according to a report in *The New York Times.* Four days later, the school responded with a new offer that increased her scholarship grant by a couple of thousand dollars. Joyce went to Harvard.

A decade ago, that sort of thing never happened—at least not at Harvard.

As a student at the University of North Carolina in the 1970s, I benefited from what was then one of the very few programs in the nation that gave generous aid without regard to need—the Morehead Scholarship program. Many of us enjoying the Morehead's free ride had, as one of my colleagues put it, "overcome every advantage" to get where we were.

But the Ivy League schools looked down their noses at the Morehead program and agreed financial aid should be based strictly on need, not merit. All the top-tier private schools, including the Ivies, met regularly in something called the "Overlap Group." They shared data on the cost of attendance and on financial aid packages, with the goal of reaching an agreement on an appropriate and common definition of financial need.

Things began to change in October 1986, however, when Princeton took a step in the direction of the Morehead program, launching a modest Scholars Program—$1,000 "research" scholarships to top students without regard for need. At a January 1987 Overlap meeting, the other schools cried foul. A Dartmouth official called Princeton's move "sophistry." Yale president Benno Schmidt wrote: "This looks like a blatant merit scholarship to me."

Two years later, the U.S. Department of Justice weighed in, with an investigation of whether the Overlap Group was a violation of the antitrust laws. In 1991, Overlap was disbanded.

The dam didn't break immediately. But then, in 1998, Princeton announced new aid formulas designed to help both middle- and lower-income families feeling squeezed by the high cost of college. Yale, Stanford, and Swarthmore all followed suit with similar program changes. In a classic case of doublespeak, Harvard resisted the new formulas but announced it was committed to making "competitively supportive offers of need-based financial aid." The bazaar was open for business.

Not everyone sees this change as a good thing. Gordon Winston, a professor of economics at Williams College, argues colleges and universities aren't well suited to the economics of the marketplace because they are "part car dealer and part church." They provide a charitable function, offering a top-flight education to students who can't afford it, paid for either by large endowments at the leading private schools or large taxpayer subsidies at the public schools.

The cost of a year at Williams, Professor Winston says, is about $65,000. Tuition is half that. And the average *price,* which is tuition adjusted for the financial aid provided by the school, is just $23,000. A similar relationship exists nationwide; the cost of a top-tier college education is three or four times more than the price at which it is sold.

Winston's worry is that as the competition to provide discounts to top students intensifies, the money available for needy students will dry up. My fear, he says, "is that need-based aid will disappear. That immediately raises the question of the social justification for these very expensive, high-cost schools, if they revert to the old pattern of being only for rich students."

But his concern won't stop the change; in the New Economy, higher education has to respond to the pressures of the market, just like any other industry.

Cyber-Education

You've heard of Harvard, but have you ever heard of the University of Phoenix? Probably not, yet it's one of the largest private universities in the nation, with more than sixty thousand students. Unlike students at most universities, these are spread out at seventy-seven different campuses and learning centers across the country, and many of them do their coursework online.

The University of Phoenix used to be derided as the McDonald's of education. But in recent years, it has gotten more serious attention. One reason: It has something many colleges and universities can only dream of—profits. And it is schools like the University of Phoenix that are moving the most quickly to bring education into the New Economy.

For years, academics have debated whether it's possible to get a good college education without the full college campus experience—the interaction between student and teacher, the intellectual experience of a lively campus, or for that matter the beer-stained carpets, stale pizzas, and obnoxious roommates. For the average eighteen-year-old, an on-campus education may still be the best way to go.

But in today's world, the demands on higher education are often coming from working adults, who are more focused in their educa-

THE WEALTH OF CHOICES

tional needs and less flexible in their lives. They are turning to both community colleges and online universities to meet those needs.

In their book *Prosperity,* my colleagues David Wessel and Bob Davis documented how community colleges are helping America's middle class retool for a changing economy. In 1996, for instance, the average graduate of a two-year community college program was making $35,201, about 20 percent more than a worker who didn't go beyond high school. Many of those graduates were people like Cornelia Wade, a forty-seven-year-old mother of nine, who was stuck in a $6-an-hour job until she enrolled in Cuyahoga Community College in Cleveland. She earned an associate degree in the spring of 1996 and immediately signed up for a nursing program at a local hospital.

With 5.5 million students enrolled in community colleges, Wessel and Davis say, those schools are "creating a growing pool of workers who have precisely the skills that command good wages in today's economy."

Even more than community colleges, though, distance learning has been the fastest-growing segment of higher education in the last few years.

Distance learning is nothing new. Penn State University started correspondence courses back in 1892. Among its students in the 1970s were two guys from Long Island named Ben Cohen and Jerry Greenfield, who paid $5 for a course in ice cream manufacture and then started Ben & Jerry's ice cream, now with 120 franchised shops across the nation. Schools have been experimenting with education by broadcast television and satellite since the 1960s.

But until recently, those experiments have done little to displace a traditional college education. For one thing, the technology was limited. On several occasions, I have lectured by videoconference to students at distant universities, and I found the experience disorienting and impersonal; no doubt the students found it more so.

Today, however, improved technology and the Internet are accelerating the move toward distance learning, much of it originating from traditional, bricks-and-mortar universities. According to Frank H. T. Rhodes, president emeritus at Cornell, the number of colleges offering Internet-based courses expanded from 93 in 1993 to 762 in 1997. A survey by International Data Corporation of college administrators concluded that 5 percent of all higher education students were enrolled in distance learning in 1998. And that figure is expected to grow to 15 percent in 2002.

To get a taste of that new world, I enrolled in Ziff Davis University, recommended by Internet entrepreneur Raul Fernandez, who founded Proxicom. I decided to audit a course on e-commerce. And I found it surprisingly instructive and lively.

For one thing, unlike correspondence courses, my ZDU course had a timetable. It began July 24 and ended on Labor Day. The course was divided into weeks, and each week came complete with a lecture, additional reading assignments, "field trips" to Internet sites, a quiz, and discussion questions. You could do the work at any time of the day or night, but you followed a syllabus that was also being followed by your classmates—allowing for more classroom interaction.

The instructor was Mickey Dodson—"to avoid any gender confusion," she wrote in her introductory lecture, "I should let you know my full name is Mickey *Marie* Dodson." She was lively and entertaining. At one point she told us how her eclectic music interests would befuddle e-commerce merchants trying to pigeonhole her tastes—"I like B.B. King and the Allman Brothers," she said, "but I *hate* the Beatles and Madonna." When directing us to pull a government document on e-commerce off the White House website, she warned us to make sure we went to WhiteHouse.gov and not WhiteHouse.org or White House.com, since the latter two sites are both pornographic.

There appeared to be about sixty people in the class, and the interaction was lively. A British woman was still a bit overwhelmed by the whole notion of e-commerce. "I cannot imagine the sales of cars or houses taking place online," she wrote. "Or cosmetics."

But in some ways, the most interesting discussions took place in the "classroom café," a site set off from the cyber-classroom, so the class could have conversations that didn't directly relate to the coursework. It was there that I got to know something about my classmates. There was David Dorsey from Ontario, who was building a website for a local historical society, and Evaristo Ferreira from Rio de Janeiro. When Pam Stevens signed on and said she was from Jefferson, Texas, another student named Ron Romanski noted that while sharing the cyber-café, he was physically just down the road, in Arlington. A number of the students had met before, in other ZDU classes. A couple had taken other courses from Mickey and enjoyed them.

And the cost? Not the $32,000 a year that the top-tier private colleges charge, but $7.95 a month.

College Savings Plans

There's no danger that Ziff-Davis University or the University of Phoenix will soon put Harvard out of business. Good brands keep their value in education, as elsewhere in the New Economy.

But these scrappy schools will teach Harvard and its hidebound colleagues the power of technology in education. Well-designed networks will eventually allow good teachers to increase their productivity ten times over.

Today's teachers often operate best in a small classroom, with no more than twenty students. The small number allows instruction to be tailored to the needs of the individual and ensures plenty of interaction between student and teacher.

Tomorrow's teacher will be able to interact more easily with two hundred students. Well-designed software will make it easier to provide individualized instruction to a multitude of students, and easier to grade multiple papers and tests. The ease of communication on the network will allow for more interaction between student and teacher, not less. When that happens, teachers will finally join the productivity revolution. And the pay of good teachers will rise, even as the cost of education falls.

In the meantime, though, the cost of higher education will continue to be an obstacle to many families. Even though the benefits are well worth the price, scrambling to pay pricy tuitions often seems to be more than many families can manage.

Student loans have become the most popular answer to that problem. Today, loans to both students and their parents are readily available. Banks, prodded by the federal government and encouraged by the record of student repayments, are now eager to lend. "More and more lenders have flooded into this market," says Ted Bracken, associate director of the Consortium on Financing Higher Education. For families that can demonstrate need, the money comes interest-free for up to eight years—until the student finishes school.

An even better approach than borrowing for college, of course, is saving for it. That's a practice few American families follow; one study found Americans save on average only about $11,000 per child, barely enough for the first semester at a private college.

But many of those who do save find it pays off. Take Keith and Sandy Wells. In 1983, they put $5,000 into ten-year, zero-coupon bonds for their four-year-old son Jeffrey. When the bonds matured a decade later, they had $20,000 to put toward Jeffrey's college tuition.

Jeffrey, then fourteen, took that money and did far better. He convinced his parents to invest in Microsoft and Intel. They agreed, and by the end of the decade his college savings had sextupled. Even after paying Boston College's steep tuition, Jeffrey has money to spare.

"I'll come out of college with more money to my name than most people owe in student loans," he says.

Of course, most people can't expect to do that well with their college savings. But it still pays to save. And in recent years, federal and state governments have been offering tax-incentives that can make college savings even more lucrative—many of them in the form of "prepaid tuition plans."

Tucked away in the fine print of the 1997 tax bill approved by Congress is a measure encouraging states to create prepaid tuition plans. The states took the hint, and the programs have popped up across the nation. Congress is now under pressure to create a similar program for private schools and to sweeten the tax benefits for both state and private programs. Most parents still haven't heard of these plans, but they could significantly alter the economics of financing higher education in the years to come.

The new state-run plans fall into two categories. The first type of plan, like the one in my home state of Maryland, provides a tuition guarantee. You pay money up front, in a lump sum or in annual payments, and the state invests your money for you and guarantees that a fixed portion of your child's tuition bill at any state university will be paid. These types of plans protect you from unexpected increases in college tuition, but don't allow you to take advantage of unexpected rises in the stock market.

The second type of plan, adopted in states like New Hampshire, Massachusetts, Delaware, and recently, California, is an investment plan. You pay up front; the money is invested for you by an organization like Fidelity Investments or TIAA-CREF and is then available for your use when your child goes to college.

New Hampshire's UNIQUE Plan, for instance, is managed by Fidelity and sets up a relatively aggressive portfolio for newborns— 88 percent equities and 12 percent bonds—and gradually shifts toward more conservative investments as the beneficiary gets older. By the time the beneficiary is in college, Fidelity splits 80 percent of the money between bonds and short-term bond and money-market funds, leaving just 20 percent in equities.

Why turn your savings over to the state instead of investing them yourself? The answer is simple: tax breaks. Earnings on the new plans accumulate free of taxes at the state or federal level. Earnings are taxed at the federal level when they are withdrawn, but at the child's lower rate. And Congress is even considering a measure that will make the earnings entirely tax-free.

Moreover, some states allow a state tax deduction for contributions to college savings plans. And the law exempts gifts of up to $50,000 made into such plans from the federal gift tax, which otherwise kicks in at $10,000 a year. That means parents and grandparents can make generous gifts to fund children's college education.

Competition is also leading states to become much more flexible in how they treat families whose children choose to attend private or out-of-state schools, or whose children may die or become disabled before going to college. There are no income or financial aid limits to worry about, as there are with various other education savings and student aid programs. No matter how affluent you are, you qualify. The only real penalties come if your child decides not to attend college—which in the New Economy is a decision he or she can scarcely afford to make.

One other drawback to the state plans is that all the money saved is counted when colleges decide how much financial aid your child is eligible for. That could reduce your aid package substantially.

As recently as 1995, there were just nine state savings plans available. But the 1997 tax law changed that, and as of mid-1999, forty-three states and the District of Columbia were offering such plans, and they will undoubtedly soon spread to all fifty states. Details vary, but you can find a description of your state's plan at collegesavings.org. And if you don't like what your state is offering, many other states will let you invest in theirs—although you're likely to lose state tax breaks.

Even without the federal government tax break, some private universities are already getting into the prepaid tuition act.

One hundred twenty-four private colleges are participating in the Consortium for Financing Higher Education, a not-for-profit tuition prepayment program scheduled to kick off at the beginning of the millennium. Under the plan, parents buy tuition certificates in whatever dollar amount they choose ($250 minimum). But there's a wrinkle: The schools are required to provide substantial discounts for the plan's participants.

The funds will be managed by TIAA-CREF. Enrollees must participate for at least three years. They have to redeem the certificates at one of the participating schools in order to realize the full value. If the coupon is redeemed at a nonparticipating private school or a public school, the refunded money is indexed to provide the same return as the interest rate or 5-year Treasury notes, or the actual rate of return if the actual return turns out to be less. Should the money be used for something other than buying an education, the saver has to pay a 10 percent penalty.

Then there's SAGE—the Savings and Growth for Education program. It was started by James Johnston, a graduate of Bucknell College, a private school in Lewisburg, Pennsylvania. In 1964 when he was attending college, he recalls, his $1,200 annual tuition was paid by his father, an $11,000-per-year mill foreman at US Steel. In 1999, Bucknell's tuition was $22,740—but mill foremen's salaries hadn't risen at nearly the same rate. So Mr. Johnston started SAGE.

Under SAGE, if you've saved for your child's college education for at least a year, the 120 participating schools will give you a discount on tuition. The discount—essentially 5 percent of your total portfolio's value, up to $50,000, varies according to how much and how long you've been saving money and is capped at $13,800. If you started saving in 1999 for your ten-year-old child and over the next eight years you accumulated $20,000, Bucknell College would give you a $2,000 annual discount on its tuition.

SAGE charges an annual $35 membership fee. An initial investment of $2,500 is required, followed by minimum investments of at least $500.

The trade-off: Once your offspring's in high school, you agree to supply certain information about him or her, such as SAT scores and extracurricular activities, to the program. SAGE passes the information along to the recruiting offices at the participating private colleges, saving them the expense of having to buy it from the Educational Testing Service or the American College Testing Program.

The College Savings Bank of Princeton, New Jersey, offers a certificate of deposit, the CollegeSure CD, which is indexed to an average tuition inflation rate. The CD is sold in tuition "units" equal to the average annual tuition of the College Board's index of five hundred private colleges. Maturities range from one to twenty-five years—but the CDs are all timed to mature on July 31, right before the start of the fall semester. The interest is subject to income tax, so you should consider opening the CD in a custodial account for your future student. That will make the first $1,400 of interest you earn either tax-free or taxable at your child's rate. Even though the CD is geared toward paying tuition, there's no formal rule requiring that you use the money for that purpose. No matter what your child decides regarding college, you'll get back the principal and interest without penalty.

Some other tools that can help you meet the high cost of college:

Education IRAs. These IRAs are also a product of the 1997 tax bill. If your income falls below certain caps—about $150,000 for joint filers—you can put $500 a year into an EIRA. There's no up-front deduction, but earnings accumulate tax free and no taxes are paid on withdrawal if earnings are used for higher education. There's pressure in Congress to expand the annual contribution limit.

One twist: You can't contribute to a state tuition plan and an EIRA in the same year without incurring a tax penalty.

Hope Scholarship Tax Credit. This program is part of Bill Clinton's legacy; it's applicable to the first two years of post-secondary education. Taxpayers can take a nonrefundable tax credit equal to 100 percent of the first $1,000 in tuition and required fees paid, plus 50 percent of the next $1,000—for a maximum yearly credit of $1,500. The credit, however, is phased out for families with incomes of more than $80,000 and for single filers with more than $40,000.

Lifetime Learning Tax Credit. Similar to the Hope provision, the Lifetime Learning Tax Credit, gives a 20 percent credit of up to $1,000 for college juniors and seniors, adults who are continuing their education, and graduate and professional students. After 2002, that's slated to rise to $2,000. The income limits are the same as for the Hope credit.

You can use the tax credits along with prepaid tuition programs, but you can't use them if any tuition is paid for with a distribution from an EIRA—unless the student waives the EIRA tax exemption.

Penalty-Free IRA Withdrawals. Starting in 1998, the tax law also allows you to take money out of your IRA for higher education expenses without paying the 10 percent penalty. Taxes, however, still have to be paid.

Grants. Don't be too quick to assume you're not eligible for financial aid. Two-thirds all students attending four-year schools are getting some form of financial aid; others could have, but didn't ask. You can start your quest by submitting the Free Application for Federal Student Aid (FAFSA) to the Department of Education. The government will then calculate how much money you'll be expected to pay towards your child's education. To apply, go to fafsa.ed.gov.

To check out privately funded scholarships—$11.2 billion worth were awarded in the 1997–98 school year—try the College Board's scholarship search site (collegeboard.org).

And here's a tip that accountants offer to self-employed people with college-bound children: Hire them. The tax benefits are huge. If you are a sole proprietor or a husband and wife partnership, the wages are exempt from social security, Medicare, and federal unemployment taxes, and your child can use the standard deduction to shelter up to $4,300 of the income from federal taxes. And you get a business deduction for money that can be used to pay college expenses—provided, of course, that your kid agrees to save it.

Six Tips for Seeking Higher Education

1. Go for the best education you or your children can get, regardless of price

The payoff for a college education in today's economy is so great that even the outsized tuitions of the elite private colleges look like a bargain when measured against the additional lifetime income they assure most of their graduates.

2. Let the tax code work for you

As lawmakers wake up to the importance of education in the New Economy, the government is adopting new tax breaks almost yearly for people saving for college. Use them.

3. Start saving now, no matter how young your child is

This was true in the old economy as well. But with the new tax breaks, the "miracle of compound interest" has never worked better. It's always wiser to let your money earn investment returns than to find yourself paying interest to someone else.

4. Haggle

Don't be snowed by the ivy; if a school wants you, many will bargain.

5. Don't be afraid to borrow

It's a better use of borrowed money than even a home mortgage. The value of that college or graduate school degree will justify the cost, many times over. But be realistic about your borrowing needs, and shop around for the best terms.

6. Don't stop learning

In the old economy, a college education was a credential. In the New Economy, it's the beginning of lifelong learning. The world is changing rapidly, and to stay afloat, you've got to stay sharp. Keep reading, keep thinking, keep questioning.

And every once in a while, go back to school!

7

Frontiers of the New Economy

Your Time and Attention Are the Scarcest Resources

The television ad showed a young couple in a romantic apartment in Paris. The man was desperately trying to persuade the woman to stay with him and build a new life in the City of Love. The woman appeared willing, except for one troubling detail:

Would she be able to choose her electric supplier?

"Whoa," said the man, taken aback. "Where do you think you are—Pennsylvania?"

Welcome to the frontiers of the New Economy. Regulated industries are crumbling, just as surely as the Berlin Wall. Free markets are taking their place. Airlines were the first to go, then trucks, then telecommunications. Now, it's electricity's turn. States like Pennsylvania, California, and Massachusetts are at the forefront in deregulating their retail electrical markets, but dozens of others are falling into place close behind. The trend is clear: In the New Economy, consumers will be able to pick their electricity supplier, just as they pick their toothpaste.

But do consumers really want to pick their own electricity supplier?

The young lady in Paris notwithstanding, few of us daydream about the merits of electrical choice. Few relish the thought of spending hours pouring over pamphlets from competing electrical suppliers or having dinner interrupted by a telemarketer pushing the latest alternative, all for a few dollars off our electric bill. Life today is complicated enough as is. Do we really need *this*?

The early returns from states experimenting with deregulation suggest many consumers are answering no. In the biggest experiment to date—California—only 1.2 percent of residential utility customers switched electrical suppliers in the first year of the program. "For an average household, I think you've got to be kind of goofy to mess around with it," fifty-nine-year-old Bob Quadross told the *San Jose Mercury News*. Besides, "nobody understands it."

Even businesses hoping to benefit from the trend have backed off. Houston's Enron Corporation spent $10 million on television advertisements and a direct mail campaign in an attempt to win over residential customers in California. But it succeeded in wooing only thirty thousand households—at a whopping cost of about $333 per household. Faced with such dismal results, the company announced it was pulling out of the residential electricity market.

Enron's failure illustrates a critical fact of life in the New Economy. Consumers are overwhelmed by the array of choices they face. Choices mean power, but consumers don't have time in their ever-more-crowded days to exercise that power. Products are cheap, information is plentiful, but there are still only twenty-four hours in a day. The scarcest resource is time and attention.

The architects of the early experiments in utility deregulation didn't understand that. They thought that if they offered the same product—electricity—at a lower price, people would buy. But it wasn't that simple.

Officials in the state of Pennsylvania thought that consumers might be reluctant to switch suppliers and worked hard to create a plan that would give consumers an incentive to do so. Still, in spite of a huge public education campaign—including the Paris lovers' ad mentioned above—only about 10 percent of the state's households had switched by the end of 1999.

In the city of Butler, for instance, just north of Pittsburgh, few residents or businesses left their traditional supplier, Allegheny Power. "I've got one or two little blurbs in the mail, but I didn't explore it," Butler resident Joe Downey told my associate, Keith Perine. "Allegheny Power has always had the reputation for being the cheapest source of power."

Bob Koehler, a retired salesman who owns and manages four hundred apartments in Butler, says none of his tenants have asked him about switching suppliers. Koehler says no one he knows has the time to research different companies in search of a few dollars in savings on their monthly bills.

Tom Gibson, an energy consultant from Greensburg, a small town southeast of Pittsburgh, signed a fifteen-month contract with QSP Energy of Illinois during the 1998 pilot program. Before the contract was up, however, QSP Energy had abandoned Pennsylvania's residential market, and Exelon Energy assumed Gibson's contract. Now, he's back with Allegheny Energy.

One of the few who have switched is Michael Stelmasczyk, a resident of the South Hills section of Pittsburgh. He moved from Duquesne Light to lower-cost Allegheny Energy and saved about

$75 a year as a result. But he's not surprised others haven't. "People are just confused by the whole process," he says.

The reluctant movement in Pennsylvania, California, and Massachusetts has slowed the pace of electricity deregulation in other states. Companies are learning that to compete successfully in this new market, they need to do more than offer a lower price. They need to recognize that consumers are facing a world of complexity and confusion and are often responding by tuning out. To win the allegiance of those consumers, companies need to first get their attention and then offer them a product that simplifies their life, rather than makes it more complex.

A Century of Regulation

But first, a little history.

In the early days of electrical power, at the end of the nineteenth century, providers did compete with one another. The results were often chaotic. Bribery of municipal officials by powerful companies seeking franchises was common. Wasteful duplication of services was rampant. In some cases, gangs from rival companies even chopped down each other's transmission poles.

Electricity had all the characteristics of a "natural monopoly"— high fixed costs to build generating capacity and a distribution system, but low marginal costs for adding each new customer to that system. As a result, the competition among companies to win monopoly status was intense, often leading to corruption. Policy makers concluded the best way to bring order to this situation was to give providers exclusive territories—to let them be monopolies— but to regulate them, so they wouldn't reap monopoly profits.

The regulatory structure that evolved was "cost plus" regulation.

Companies were allowed to recover their costs and take a reasonable profit on top. But that structure also led to prices for electricity that varied widely from one utility to the next. Huge investments in nuclear power in the 1970s and 1980s only worsened the problem; nuclear plants turned out to be enormously costly and not very efficient.

By the 1990s, consumers in Pittsburgh were paying nearly double what the folks paid in Uniontown, just fifty miles away. And consumers in New York State, which had the most expensive electricity in the nation, were paying on average three times as much as consumers in the State of Washington, who benefited from cheap hydropower generated by government-built dams.

The demand for change came from big businesses in high-cost regions. A group called the Electricity Consumers Resource Council, representing thirty-five large corporations, including Ford and General Motors and the major oil, chemical, and steel firms, was formed in 1976. These companies say that together, they consume 6 percent of the nation's electricity in their manufacturing processes. And they are tired of paying high, regulated rates.

Technology changed too. New combined-cycle gas turbines developed in the last decade enable relatively small generating plants to be more cost-effective than the generating plants of old. That has increased the demands from businesses for access to lower-priced power.

As a result, the regulatory regime for electricity began to crumble. The wholesale market was deregulated in 1996.

Some liberal analysts, like Amory Lovins at the Rocky Mountain Institute, argued that the process ought to stop with wholesale deregulation. Allowing each household and business to choose its own power supplier, he feared, would enable big companies to corner the cheapest power sources. But the momentum for deregulation was unstoppable.

The idea was to separate the *generation* of electricity from the *distribution*. Distribution would still be handled by the local monopoly. But if consumers were free to choose the company that generated their electricity, power suppliers would have to become more efficient and lower their prices.

One major sticking point in all of this was the transition—how to get from a regulated world to a deregulated one—a problem not unlike the costly transitions of socialist economies to capitalist ones in Eastern Europe.

In particular, the problem was who was going to pick up the bill for all the money wasted on nuclear power plants—estimated at $100 billion or more. Deregulation advocates said utilities and their shareholders ought to pay for their mistakes, like any other company. But the utilities argued that regulators had approved—and in many cases encouraged—those costly investments and that ratepayers, or taxpayers, ought to pay the bill.

With considerable political clout, utilities did a good job winning the argument. Ratepayers in both California and Pennsylvania must pay a "competitive transition charge" to finance the wasted investments of the old utilities, even if they switch to a new provider. That sharply reduces the benefits to consumers of switching.

As a result, businesses in deregulated states have been quick to find new suppliers. But ordinary consumers haven't.

"It gets down to economies of scale," says Dave Potter of New Energy Ventures, a Los Angeles firm that is servicing twelve hundred large commercial and industrial accounts in Pennsylvania, but has opted out of the residential market. "It's difficult for us to bring significant value to residential customers at a reasonable cost of doing business."

Getting Their Attention

Still, slowly, it is happening. Over time, three very different but successful strategies are emerging from the early chaos of deregulation in Pennsylvania. Each of these strategies plays to the consumers' desire for simplicity and for relationships they can trust. And each says something about the direction of consumer services in the New Economy.

Branding

The biggest surprise of deregulation is that among consumers who have switched, many have switched to higher-priced electricity, not lower-priced.

The reason? A company called Green Mountain Energy Resources.

Based in Vermont, Green Mountain is the first to succeed at "branding" electricity. It has offered consumers a variety of types of power that are generated in ways that are benign for the environment, either through natural gas plants, hydroelectric dams, or solar panels and windmills. Customers who sign up with Green Mountain feel they are helping the environment by steering clear of dangerous nuclear power or dirty coal-generated power. They trust Green Mountain both to do what's right for the environment and to give them a fair price—although a higher price than they could get elsewhere.

The company offers a variety of energy "blends." The least expensive is Eco Smart, which is 1 percent renewable energy, such as solar and wind energy, and 99 percent "cleaner burning natural gas and hydro power." A more expensive product is Enviro Blend, which offers 50 percent renewable energy and 50 percent natural gas and hydropower. And the most expensive is Nature's Choice, which is 100 percent renewable. On the company's website, GreenMountain.com, you can quickly check how prices compare with your current service. If Penn Power is your current provider and you pay $100 a month, for instance, Eco Smart will cost $107, Enviro Blend will cost $116, and Nature's Choice will cost $122.

Green Mountain has been competing for business aggressively in Pennsylvania, with television ads, billboards, and an Internet campaign. In the fall of 1998, the company even hosted a "Know Your Power" music festival in Philadelphia, where musicians such as James Taylor, Kenny Loggins, and Shawn Colvin performed for more than fifty thousand people.

The results have been surprising. The company has signed up more than eighty thousand customers in Pennsylvania and California and says that 30 percent of the Pennsylvanians who have changed their electric supplier have chosen Green Mountain. That still makes them something of a "boutique" in the electricity business. But their ability to establish a premium brand has gotten the attention of other suppliers.

In the end, what Green Mountain did was simplify the buying decision for some consumers. Rather than scour brochures to find the cheapest power, Green Mountain's customers decided they were willing to pay more as long as they were paying more for a good reason and were working with a company they could trust.

Other companies are trying the same approach, with some success. Conectiv, the former Delmarva Power & Light Co., has garnered more than ten thousand customers for its two "blends" of either 50 percent or 100 percent renewable energy.

Pooling

In Pennsylvania, few companies have been willing to spend the money to win over residential customers one by one. The costs of direct mail and telephone campaigns are simply too high, and the potential profits too thin. But when approached by a pool of ready-made customers, the companies are willing to deal.

That's the lesson learned by Chris Lochner, the manager of Hampton Township, a community of 6,185 households spread out along the Pennsylvania Turnpike, fourteen miles north of Pittsburgh. He persuaded thousands of the township's households to form a purchasing pool in order to get a better deal on their electricity than the 4.505 cents per kilowatt-hour that Duquesne Light was charging them.

"Unless you're a huge corporation, it's hard to save money," Lochner explained. He went to several different suppliers, offering to line up his residents for them in exchange for a cheaper rate. Many of the companies were interested, but Lochner found few that were willing to negotiate a contract locking in a low rate for an entire year.

Finally, Allegheny Energy told Lochner that if he signed up between 500 and 3,000 households, they would offer a rate of 4 cents per kilowatt-hour, slightly cheaper than their usual rate of 4.1 cents. If he got more than 3,000 households to join the pool, Allegheny Energy promised to come down to 3.95 cents.

Lochner sent out a mailing on the township's letterhead, along with Allegheny Energy's logo, making Hampton Township the first residential buying pool in the state. As of last summer, Lochner estimated that 3,100 township households were in the pool at the 3.95-cent rate, a savings of as much as $85 a year for some residents.

Lochner saved his constituents even more money by negotiating a 3.7-cent rate for the township's own electric bills, which means the township's taxpayers will collectively save another $25,000 per year.

Lochner's campaign spurred Allegheny Energy to embark on a campaign to sign up aggregated pools in other townships and municipalities in largely rural western Pennsylvania. The company used to buy expensive television advertising to try to convince skeptical Pennsylvania consumers to switch suppliers, with little success. Now, company spokesmen travel to city council meetings to persuade local governments to partner with them to offer residents a better deal. Everyone wins: Local governments lend their credibility to Allegheny Energy. And consumers get a deal they feel they can trust because their local leaders have endorsed it. In Collier Township, southwest of Pittsburgh, for instance, one quarter of the township's 2,400 households have joined an Allegheny Energy pool.

The lesson: Consumers can have more power if they pool their resources. In the New Economy, a collection of ready and willing customers is a valuable asset.

Bundling

Companies are learning that in the New Economy, physical products—in this case electricity—become commodities, offering only slim profits to those who produce them. The key to success is not only producing electricity, but having a relationship with consumers. In a deregulated electricity market, a loyal base of customers is a more valuable asset than the generating plant.

But how do you build a loyal base of customers? One approach gaining adherents is "bundling"—providing a package of services that allows people to simplify their lives with one-stop shopping.

Sanjay Chopra, a businessman in the small western Pennsylvania town of Mars, is at the front end of this trend. He's using the Internet to aggregate pools of residential and business customers. Chopra eventually hopes to expand his website, electricitychoice.com, to offer aggregated consumers natural gas, telephone, and health care providers.

"Our grand vision is to sell convenience in the marketplace," Chopra says.

Conectiv, the Delaware-based utility, is trying the same thing on a larger scale. The company is looking to sell electricity, natural gas, plumbing, heating, ventilation, and telecommunications services, all in a package.

"We're trying to move away from just the power-company and energy image and redefine ourselves as a provider of vital services," Howard Cosgrove, chairman of Conectiv, told my *Journal* colleague Kathryn Kranhold. To push the idea, the utility hired Jason Alexander, formerly of TV's *Seinfeld,* as its pitchman, and bought television ads during the Super Bowl.

Scott McDonald, who runs the energy and telecommunications

business for Proxicom, the Internet firm, suggests utilities may want to go into the appliance business as well. In the future, appliances are likely to be equipped with computers and connect to the Internet so that you can, for instance, turn on your oven from the office to cook a chicken before you come home. That would give electrical utilities a natural entrée into the high-tech world.

In any event, says McDonald, bundling is clearly the future. It's what consumers want—a company that will promise them good products and services at a good price with a minimum of hassle. "Everybody agrees we are going to get there. It is going to happen," he says. "It's just a question of time."

A California company, Utility.com, is promising residential and small-business customers in that state 7 percent savings on their electric bills and the convenience of online billing. Customers can pay by credit card or electronic funds transfer. The company is planning to enter the markets in other deregulated states as well. Plans include up-to-the-minute meter readings available online: Utility.com installs a meter that reports itself electronically to the website so customers can log on and watch their meters whirring away.

What does all this mean for you?

Well, first, don't be discouraged by the complexity and confusion caused by the deregulation of electricity. Like previous deregulation efforts, this one puts the consumer in charge. The power has shifted from the regulators to you. It may take companies a while to figure out how to give you something you want. But you can take comfort from the fact that they are struggling mightily to figure that out. In the old days, their goal was to keep the regulators happy; today, it's to keep *you* happy.

If you live in a state that's deregulating and you are eager to get the most out of deregulation right away, then shop around. Odds are, you can find a better deal than the one you have. And if the deal doesn't seem good enough, look for a way to create a purchasing pool, through your town, your neighborhood, your PTA, or some other organization, and bargain for more.

And if all that seems like more trouble than it's worth, then just sit back and wait. Change is happening rapidly, and businesses are focused more than ever before on this goal: providing value to the consumer. Exactly how they'll do that remains unclear. Maybe a company will offer to negotiate the best deals on your behalf for all your household utilities and then combine them all into one easy-to-pay bill. Maybe someone will offer you a package deal to provide electricity and upgrade and network your household appliances at the same time.

But eventually, some one will come up with a way to give you the value you want. Because in the New Economy, you have the power.

8

Working in the
New Economy

You Are Your Own Brand

At the beginning of the classic 1950s movie *The Man in the Gray Flannel Suit*, Gregory Peck is riding on a commuter train with an older gentleman who mentions that there might be a job opening in public relations at his corporation, United Broadcasting.

"I don't know anything about public relations," Peck says.

"Who does?" the man replies. "You've got a clean shirt. You bathe every day. What else is there to it?"

That was corporate America, circa 1955. If you dressed well and played by the rules, the company would take care of you. ("We always give the new man the prettiest secretary," Peck's new boss explains his first day on the job. "It makes things easier for the breaking-in period.")

Paternalism was the order of the day. The depression and the war had created a longing for security, a longing for protection from what President Franklin D. Roosevelt had called "the winds of change and the hurricanes of disaster." The government responded by creating the social security program and by regulating many essential industries. Big corporations danced to the tune as well, building a protective, if sometimes stifling, cocoon for their employees. The job "market" was something for people seeking jobs; once you found one with a big company, you were largely shielded from market forces. And when you retired, you got a nice pension and a gold watch.

Now fast-forward the videotape to 1999. IBM, once the ultimate in flannel-suit employers, is engulfed in controversy for adopting a new "cash balance" pension plan. The old plan was designed to lock employees in until their retirement; most of its benefits accrued in the final five to ten years of an employee's working life. The new plan seems designed to push old-timers out. Benefits accrue more quickly to young employees and can be carried from job to job; but old-timers could lose 20 to 50 percent of their benefits. Not surprisingly, the older employees rose up in revolt and forced the company to offer them a choice of plans. But the brouhaha illustrates how dramatically the world of work has changed.

What's happening here is what's happening everywhere in the New Economy: The workplace is becoming a marketplace. In the old days, pay levels, benefits, and promotions within American corporations were determined as much by social convention as by supply and demand. The flannel-suit man saw his pay rise as he grew older, when he got married, when he had children, or as he racked up more years with the company. Disparities in pay were kept within limits; large pay differentials among colleagues, or a big gap between the pay of the worker and the boss, were seen as fomenting workplace unrest. Firings were reserved for those who committed gross acts of incompetence or insubordination.

But the modern worker faces a ruthless, market-driven world that compensates people according to the market's valuation of their worth. Young employees may earn far more than their older colleagues, if they bring skills or talents in hot demand. Pay disparities in the workplace are frequent and huge. The best way for someone to get a pay raise today is to show that someone else is willing to pay more. And even the most conscientious employee can end up on the street if he or she doesn't have something to contribute. Christmas bonuses, once commonplace in half of large U.S. employers, are now found in barely a third.

Much ink has been spilled in recent years on the rise of the contingent workforce—temporary workers, consultants, or job-hoppers who float from one employer to the next. And to be sure, in 1997, 30 percent of the U.S. workforce was employed in situations that weren't regular full-time jobs. Manpower Inc. employs more people in the course of a year than any other private employer.

But the change in work arrangements has gone far deeper than just the contingent, or free agent, workforce. It permeates the workplace. Even those who've been at the same employer their entire working lives recognize the change. Loyalty and security are gone; Adam Smith has taken their place.

Sound scary? For many, it is. Certainly the risks are greater than they were in the old days.

But here's the upside: The rewards are greater too. If you make yourself valuable, make yourself indispensable, you can be rewarded accordingly.

In fact, the secret to success in the New Economy is to think of yourself as an entrepreneur, regardless of what you do. Think of yourself as a product that is being offered in the marketplace for labor. You are the product manager, who works to refine the product and make sure it is desirable and valuable. And you are the marketing director, who works to make sure the marketplace appreciates that value.

The farsighted business consultant Tom Peters made the argument best in an article he wrote for *FastCompany* magazine:

> It's time for me—and you—to take a lesson from the big brands, a lesson that's true for anyone who's interested in what it takes to stand out and prosper in the new world of work. Regardless of age, regardless of position, regardless of the business we happen to be in, all of us need to understand the importance of branding. We are CEOs of our own companies: Me Inc. To be in business today, our most important job is to be head marketer for the brand called You.

That means figuring out what your special strengths are, figuring out what your interests are, and developing them and marketing them. It means working on ways to distinguish yourself from the pack—to show how you are different, and better, than brand X. It means looking for ways to get people interested in what you are doing, doing things that others want to be a part of, creating a buzz. As Peters puts it, it's not who's got the biggest office or who's got the fanciest title. It's who's making the most significant contribution, who's getting noticed or cited by others, who's creating value.

A career today, Peters explains, isn't a ladder. It's "a portfolio of projects that teach you new skills, gain you new expertise, develop new capabilities, grow your colleague set, and constantly reinvent you as a brand."

That may sound a bit selfish; but remember, it's the pursuit of self-interest that in Adam Smith's world leads to the best outcome for society. And Peters certainly isn't suggesting workers ignore the interests of their colleagues or their employers; on the contrary, he thinks teamwork is critical in the New Economy, and being a good teammate is as well. But if you develop your own skills, you make yourself a more valuable teammate and a more valuable employee.

Most American workers haven't yet caught up to the new reality. They're inclined to think a job's a job, and if they do what they are told, and do it well, they'll survive. Michael Hammer and James Champy capture this old mindset in their book *Reengineering the Corporation:*

- My boss pays my salary . . . the real objective is to keep the boss happy.
- I'm just a cog in the wheel: My best strategy is to keep my head down and not make waves.
- The more direct reports I have, the more important I am; the one with the biggest empire wins.
- Tomorrow will be just like today; it always had been.

But tomorrow won't be like today, and today isn't like yesterday. Your boss may be gone, and your big staff may be, too. The way to survive is not to avoid making waves, but to *make waves*. As Hammer and Champy put it, in the New Economy "showing up is no accomplishment." You get paid for the value you create.

Look around you, and you'll see people who are profiting from the new reality. They've learned new skills, polished old ones, and pursued their passionate interests, and they have been rewarded as a result. For me, even this book is a means of polishing my "brand"; I've seen things, learned things, and met people I might never have encountered in the course of my job as Washington bureau chief of *The Wall Street Journal.* And I've made myself more valuable to the *Journal,* and to others, as a result.

If you think about your work life in this way, you'll see that these revolutionary changes, while often frightening, are also empowering. You are the master of your fate; you are the architect of your future. Have at it. There's certainly a greater chance than in the past that you will fail. But there's also a greater chance that you'll succeed beyond your dreams.

A Revolution in the Making

The new world of work has been a long time coming.

My father was a Westinghouse man. He grew up in the shadow of a giant Westinghouse plant in Pittsburgh and began sweeping floors there as a teenager. After the war, he earned an engineering degree at the University of Kansas courtesy of the GI bill, then went into sales, selling Westinghouse electrical equipment to regulated utilities. Every two or three years the company would ask him to move to a new location, and he would agree. When my brothers and I were born, he would ask for more money and the company would agree. Everything in our house was made by Westinghouse; I never used a General Electric appliance until I went to college.

In the 1960s, though, that world began to change. Conventional wisdom credits a resurgent conservative movement for bringing down the corporate welfare state; but in fact, it was the sixties student movement that started the ball rolling. At the core of that

movement was radical individualism. Paternalism in all its mani-
festations was the enemy. The man in the gray flannel suit may have
been exactly who Bob Dylan had in mind when he sang out to
"mothers and fathers throughout the land" to get out of the new
road if they can't "lend a hand."

My father was no sixties radical, but he left Westinghouse in 1967
to go into business for himself. He became an early "free agent," representing other electrical equipment makers as a manufacturers'
representative. Westinghouse had asked him to move one more
time, and he finally said no.

The rebellion of the 1960s was followed by the economic tur-
moil of the 1970s. Inflation hit many comfortable American companies hard. And global competition began to break up cozy
oligopolies. General Motors, Ford, and Chrysler could divide the
market pretty neatly among themselves; but Toyota, Honda, and
Nissan were another matter. The Japanese invasion sent many
American companies back to the drawing boards, to rethink what
they were doing.

The irony, of course, was that Japanese companies were far more
paternalistic than American companies had ever been. During my
year in Tokyo, my friend Yasushi Yuge and I would often talk about
how different our work lives were. I had quit the *Congressional
Quarterly* to come to Japan because the magazine refused to give me
a leave. Now my editor was bidding to get me back at a much higher
salary. Yuge, on the other hand, was eager to work overseas, but felt
he was at the mercy of his employer. If he quit, the company would
certainly never take him back; nor could he go to work for another
major Japanese paper, since all would view him as disloyal.

In the early 1980s, many American intellectuals and business

consultants admiringly advocated a Japanese-style "lifetime employment" system for American companies. But the forces of
change were all working in the opposite direction. Technology was
one of those forces; computers were coming into widespread use,
eliminating whole layers of jobs and radically changing others.
Globalization and deregulation were increasing the competitive
pressures on companies to become more efficient. The declining
power of unions, symbolized by Ronald Reagan's breaking of the air
traffic controllers' strike in 1981, made it easier for companies to
shed unwanted employees. And a wave of corporate restructuring
in the eighties and nineties made it almost mandatory that they do
so, in order to remain in favor with financial markets. For a while,
"Chainsaw Al" Dunlap became an admired business icon for the
ruthlessness with which he dismissed his employees at Scott Paper
and, later, Sunbeam.

As a result, the workplace was transformed. The attitude is no
longer familial; it is strictly business. I will work for you as long as it
suits my interest; you will keep me employed as long as it suits
yours. You don't pay more than is necessary; I won't take less than I
can get elsewhere. And the workplace is no longer hierarchical either. At the modern corporation, there is no career ladder; instead,
there is something more like the ubiquitous network. You look for a
place where you can plug in and perform a valuable service, or you
look for projects. Some services and projects are more valuable than
others, and some workers are more valuable than others. The person next to you might earn two, three, or ten times what you do—
something virtually unheard of in the old days. But always, it's the
market that decides.

To see how significant those changes have been in just one generation, consider the lives of Bob Kinzer and his daughter, Kathy LaFollett.

Kinzer put in thirty-six years at Black Brothers Company, an industrial machine manufacturer in Mendota, Illinois. For him, the loyalty between employer and employee was such a natural bond that he never gave it much thought.

"You've got to have loyalty to the company that you work for," Kinzer says. "I never stopped to ask myself 'What am I doing here?' "

He began as a draftsman in 1963, then moved up to customer service manager. The company is small, with about ninety employees, a number that hasn't changed much during Kinzer's time there. It's a family-owned firm that Kinzer says "really cares about the employees." He has had the same fee-for-service health care plan his entire career. Black Brothers also sponsors long-term disability coverage and a life insurance policy. Annual golf and bowling tournaments, and a company picnic every summer, keep Kinzer and his coworkers close.

As with any business, Black Brothers has gone through its share of downturns. But Kinzer says he's never been worried about losing his job. Rather than lay anyone off, the company puts everyone on a four-day workweek until things get better. When he retires this year, Kinzer will take advantage of Black Brothers' pension program.

"A job is a job," Kinzer says. "If it pays well, you should just stay with it."

Kinzer's daughter, on the other hand, has already held five different jobs at the age of thirty-six. She had been a freelance court reporter, an illustrator, and a television producer before starting her own staffing firm in 1997. Married and the mother of two children, LaFollett has always paid for her own health and retirement plans.

"I don't ever look to a company to make sure I can retire," LaFollett says. "That's my job."

LaFollett respects the loyalty her father felt for his employer—but she has never felt or expected the same kind of loyalty in her own career.

"My loyalty is to my family foremost," says LaFollett. "My employers have been a vehicle to meet the demands of my family—nothing more."

The dramatic changes in the workplace that separate Kinzer and LaFollett have been wrenching ones for many workers. The median income of American families doubled during the first twenty-five years after World War II, even after adjusting for inflation. But between 1973 and 1997, median family income rose only 9 percent.

Moreover, that rise in income occurred only because many women went to work. Families with one worker lost ground over the last quarter century. The families that saw sizable gains were those with two earners. Hours worked outside the home by married women aged twenty-five to fifty-four rose more than 30 percent between 1979 and 1997.

Those averages belie another trend of the last quarter of the twentieth century: increased inequality. Family income for the most affluent fifth of the population actually rose 22 percent between 1973 and 1997, while income for the least affluent fifth dropped 6 percent. The protected labor markets of the 1950s and 1960s had a socialist-style effect on workers' pay, keeping a lid on the earnings of those at the top and a floor under those at the bottom. But in the 1980s and 1990s, market forces eroded those conventions. The floor dropped, and the lid was lifted. The most spectacular illustration of that is seen in what happened to CEO pay. In 1965, the typical CEO made twenty times the pay of the average worker; in 1997, the CEO made more than a hundred times the pay of the average worker.

In the meantime, workers' fears of losing their jobs rose sharply, and for good reason. In 1979, roughly half of male workers had held the same job for ten years or more; in 1996, that percentage had dropped to 40 percent. Even in good times, jobs were at risk. AT&T, for instance, cut forty thousand positions in 1995, a year in which it reported profits of $1.2 billion.

Experience counts for less in the New Economy. The economist Lester Thurow argues that even though American men are living longer, they are hitting their peak earning years between thirty-five and forty-five, instead of between forty-five and fifty-five. That adds even more insecurity for older workers.

Add to that the fact that pension benefits and health benefits cover fewer people today than they did twenty years ago. In 1979, 51 percent of all workers were covered by pension plans. In 1996, that figure had dropped to 47 percent. The trend in health benefits was similar, falling from 70 percent in 1979 to 63 percent in 1996, with men registering a sharper decline than women.

But take a deep breath. After that flood of dismal statistics, here's the most surprising thing of all:

In spite of these changes, most American workers embrace the New Economy. They recognize the risks, but welcome the opportunities.

A 1998 survey by Mark Penn, pollster to President Clinton,

found that 68 percent of Americans felt the United States was gaining ground in the New Economy, and 57 percent felt they personally
were gaining. Only 6 percent thought they had been hurt by
changes in technology, and only 16 percent thought they had been
hurt by increasing trade and globalization. Among parents, 75 percent thought changes in technology would make the lives of their
children better, and 65 percent thought trade and globalization
would do the same.

That optimism may partly reflect the fact that some of the dismal trends of the last quarter-century have turned around in recent
years. Since 1996, the productivity and wages of American workers,
adjusted for inflation, have been on the upswing, as the benefits of
technology and corporate retooling have started to kick in. Moreover, wage gains have been even bigger at the bottom of the income
scale than elsewhere.

The optimism also reflects the traditional willingness on the
part of many Americans to accept greater risks in return for greater
potential gains. It's that adventuresome spirit that leads so many
Americans to play the lottery, invest in stocks, participate in extreme sports, or launch entrepreneurial ventures. They've been
willing to give up the security of the old economy in return for the
greater rewards of the new one.

The clearest example of this is in the software industry, where
software "gypsies" float from job to job, building their own skills
and seeking a big payoff. In the 1960s, the nation had less than five
thousand professional computer programmers; today, there are 1.3
million, and the technology section of the Sunday classified-job ads
is growing to doorstop proportions. Workers in Silicon Valley

change jobs at twice the national average. The expansion of the high-technology sector and low-single-digit unemployment rates mean that good people are harder and harder to find.

For those with the right skills, the compensation has never been better. A host of new benefits have sprung up alongside the traditional medical-dental-pension troika. The number of employers offering flex-time, on-site child care, health club memberships, domestic partner benefits, long-term care insurance, and even pet care is steadily growing. Corporate concierge services do everything from dry-cleaning your clothes to walking your dog to framing your artwork. Relocation packages, cell phones, laptops, and even clothing allowances are now standard at many companies.

Net2000, a telecommunications company based in Herndon, Virginia, has a "Car in Every Garage" incentive program that grants three-year leases of luxury BMWs for outstanding employees who have been with the company at least two years. "We want our employees to astonish our customers," says Net2000's chief executive, Charlie Thomas, "and to have fun doing it." The company figures that its leasing costs are outweighed by a reduction in the recruiting fees it pays.

And in the high-tech business, stock options have become the Holy Grail. Workers dream of wealth never before imagined by rank and file workers—and sometimes, they get it. In northern Virginia, for instance, literally thousands of new millionaires have been created by America Online Inc., which saw its stock price go up 700-fold after going public in 1992 and has had the habit of handing out stock options as if they were keys to the restroom.

Most workers, of course, can never hope to get rich off of stock options. And the New Economy is bound to create tragic disappointment among many who did nurture that hope and didn't insist on competitive pay and benefits as a result.

But the work experience of the software gypsies offers lessons for others in the New Economy. These workers show surprisingly little loyalty to the company, but work long hours to build their own skills and improve the products they are working on. As one software manager told business professor Rosabeth Moss Kantor: "The thing I always tell everybody is that while we want our company to succeed, more importantly, we want the platform that we're running on to succeed. So if this company crashes and burns, we can go somewhere else and leverage what we did here."

Polishing Your Brand

How can you minimize the risks and maximize the opportunities in the new world of work? For starters, ask yourself the following ten questions about your current job or any job you may be considering.

1. Is this a job that allows me to make a real contribution?

In the new marketplace, you get paid for the value you create. A job that offers a lot of money for little work might once have seemed a dream. But in today's ruthless market, it's a dead end. Instead, you should be in a job that makes you feel like you are contributing, and in which your contributions are appreciated. The greater the contribution, the greater the ultimate rewards.

Another way to think about this is to ask yourself the question: If the company were taken over tomorrow, would I be able to justify my job to the new employers?

2. Will I learn something from this job that advances my career?

In the New Economy, employers can't offer you loyalty, but they can offer you new skills. If you view your work as a simple trade-off— your time and effort in return for their money—you'll wake up one day and find yourself out of a job and out of luck. But if you view it as a constant investment in your own skills and potential, your value will rise and you need never fear being obsolete. Think of each job as being a stepping stone to the next. When this one's over, you don't want to feel you've been drained; you want to feel that you are new and improved.

3. Is this employer willing to invest in my education and training?

According to *Fortune* magazine, the one hundred best companies to work for in America gave their employees an average of forty-three hours of training in 1998. Computer Associates in Islandia, New York, enrolls new hires in a thirty-two-month course in software technology and continues their training at a rate of one hundred or more hours a year. (You can check out how much training each of *Fortune*'s "100 Best" provides at Fortune.com.)

Tuition reimbursement plans, which some companies dropped during the cost cutting of the 1980s and 1990s, have been making a comeback as employers try to stay competitive. The better plans reimburse you for all of your tuition and fees, as long as you keep your grades up.

Keith Perine's brother Mark provides a classic example of how to use tuition benefits. He started working for Cable and Wireless, the British telecommunications firm, in 1991, and he used the company's tuition reimbursement program to pay for technical training at Northern Virginia Community College and a bachelor's degree in information systems from American University. Last July, Mark got a new job at Bell Atlantic, and he is using Bell Atlantic's tuition reimbursement plan to earn his executive MBA from George Washington University.

4. Does this job give me the freedom to do what I think is best?

Workplaces in the old economy tended to be top-down hierarchies, with clear job descriptions. You could usually figure out the rankings just by looking around—whose cubicle walls were higher, who had the corner office. The offices with windows were coveted real estate. The oldest-looking guy in a suit was usually the one in charge.

In the New Economy, successful companies are pushing authority and accountability down the line. Many employers have changed their workplace cultures by instituting employee-management committees, quality circles, and employee teams to give workers a greater say in the decision making and to spur them to work better.

SEI Investments, a financial services firm headquartered in Oaks, Pennsylvania, has instituted a "fluid leadership" model that has helped its stock price triple over the last three years. The offices on SEI's campus have no walls, no secretaries, and no human resources department. The work is divided among 140 teams, some permanent, some that form and disband according to the needs of the moment. To help make movement easier, all of the office furniture is on wheels.

If a company hasn't moved out of the old economy, chances are it's not the right place to get you ready for the new one.

5. Are the health benefits adequate?

Most people don't think much about health benefits until they get sick. By then, it's too late. Take a close look at the company's health plan, and make sure you know what it covers and what it doesn't. If you are an unmarried male, the fact that it won't pay for a mammography needn't bother you too much. But if you have young children, the absence of a dental plan with good orthodontia coverage could become a problem.

If the job comes with no health benefits—amazingly, many do—you should chalk that up as a sign of an employer's lack of commitment to employees. You should also make sure you know how much it will cost you to buy coverage on your own.

Many employers now offer medical "flexible spending accounts" that allow you to set aside anywhere from $2,000 to $5,000 in pre-tax dollars for medical expenses that aren't covered by the health care plan. These are particularly useful if you can foresee large medical expenses in an upcoming year—for instance, from a pregnancy or from major cosmetic surgery or orthodontic work.

6. What if I become disabled?

In the New Economy, you spend your career building human capital, making yourself eagerly sought after in the job market. So, you don't want a sudden disability to leave you in the lurch. Look for long-term disability coverage, which is offered by many employers if you are incapacitated for more than six months. The standard level of coverage is 60 percent of your pre-disability income, usually up to $15,000 per month.

More than half of the employers who offer long-term disability coverage pay for it themselves—but one in three employers require you to bear all of the costs. If your employer doesn't offer disability coverage, you can make a disability insurance claim to the Social Security Administration, which pays benefits according to a formula based on your lifetime average earnings. But the payments are slim; you may want to supplement that with disability insurance of your own.

7. Are the retirement benefits adequate?

They probably won't be. We'll deal with the challenges of retirement in the New Economy in Chapter 11. But no matter how young you are, take a close look at the retirement plan.

The old economy's defined-benefit pension programs, paid for entirely by employers and based on service longevity, are disappearing. They're giving way to defined-contribution retirement plans, such as 401(k) programs that employees contribute to and that aren't predicated on length of service. But defined-benefit plans haven't disappeared yet—in a 1999 survey, 71 percent of the employers responding said they still offered them alongside the newer retirement benefits. Defined-benefit programs typically pay an average based on your annual salary during your last few years with the company, with a vesting period of five years.

The 401(k) is by far the most popular of the new retirement plans. Employers usually match 50 percent of their employees'

401(k) contributions to a tax-deferred investment account. Employees are usually vested after one year on the job.

8. Will I make contacts that will help lead me to other jobs?

The best jobs aren't listed in the classifieds or posted on Monster.com. They're passed around by word of mouth. You need a job that will help you build a network of contacts—not only professionally but personally—and keep it active. Treat everyone you meet as a potential employer; your boss's administrative assistant might one day become a headhunter with a lucrative job offer.

Even when you're not contemplating a job change, your network will help you keep up with developments in your field so you can do your existing job well.

You can expand your network on the Internet, through corporate alumni clubs that bring together hundreds of former employees of corporations such as IBM and Compaq. The clubs, many of which have mission statements and logos, perpetuate fraternities of former colleagues who give each other career advice and job leads.

9. Do I get stock options?

Stock options, the boutique perquisite of the New Economy, give employees the right to buy company stock at a fixed price, irrespective of its selling price on the open market. The vesting period is usually five years, but can be as few as three and as many as ten. Formerly an incentive offered only to top management, options now are being broadly distributed to give workers another incentive to work hard and stay on the job for at least a few years. The number of major employers offering broad-based options more than doubled between 1993 and 1999.

There are two kinds of options. Incentive options receive the more favorable tax treatment. There is no tax when the options are executed, and any appreciation of the stock over the "strike price" is taxed at the low capital gains rate. When nonqualified options are executed, you must pay ordinary income tax on the difference between the "strike price" and the market value at the time they are executed. You should evaluate stock options according to the vesting period—the shorter, the better—and the overall health of the company. Research the company's health just as if you were buying its stock as an outside investor—which leads to the next question, below.

And don't be bamboozled by a company's promise to make you rich with stock options, in lieu of fair pay. A bird in the hand is still worth two in the bush.

10. Is the company healthy? Is it growing?

Prospective employers do plenty of research on you; to protect yourself, you ought to do just as much on them. Think of your job as an investment; is this a company you would want to own a piece of?

Your human network can come into play when you're researching a company. If you know people who work there, ask them about their experiences. If you don't know someone who works there, find out whether anyone in your network does. If the company has an alumni club, tap into the sentiments of the ex-employees. They'll rarely sugarcoat a bad corporate experience.

Also, you can research the company at WSJ.com or

Wetfeet.com. Wetfeet offers the inside scoop on jobs in different industries. If you're curious about what it's like to work at *The Wall Street Journal,* for instance, Wetfeet will give you its spin. The good part: "Captains of industry and PR people earning three times your salary will actively seek to curry favor." And the bad part: "Think of the worst snobs you know. Journalists and the lonely few still publishing worthy books are much worse than that."

THE GLOBAL JOB BAZAAR

With the advent of the Internet, the job market, like so many other markets, has gone global.

As of January 1999, 45 percent of the Fortune Global 500 companies were using the online job market to hire employees. Employers are expected to spend $1 billion a year or more posting want ads in cyberspace in the next few years.

Hundreds of job sites have sprung up, but the behemoth of the group is Monster.com, which began as a modest cyberspace job board at a Boston ad agency in 1994. The site's popularity has grown with the help of a memorable television campaign, launched during the 1999 Super Bowl, in which cherubic children deadpanned their career goals. "I want to claw my way to middle management," said one. "I want to be fired on a whim," said another.

In July 1999, Monster.com launched an experiment to create a true auction market for workers. You could post your résumé, along with a "talent profile" that highlights your qualifications and salary requirements, and see what employers would bid for your services.

Besides searching jobs and picking up career tips, visitors to Monster.com can do side-by-side demographic and cost-of-living comparisons of many U.S. cities. The "Insurance Professor" tells you all about homeowner's and automobile insurance. You can even compare school districts according to student-teacher ratios and whether there are computers in the elementary school classrooms.

Dozens of newspapers across the country have joined forces to sponsor CareerPath.com, a no-nonsense job site that lets you post your résumé, look for a job, or even take a "business clothing IQ test."

9

Investing in the New Economy

Everyone's an Expert

On June 1, 1999, another Berlin Wall fell.

Until that day, Merrill Lynch stood as a proud symbol of the notion that you needed an expert to navigate the stock market. The firm had resisted the rush to online trading. Just a few months earlier, John "Launny" Steffens, Merrill's brokerage chief, had publicly declared that "the do-it-yourself model of investing, centered on Internet trading, should be regarded as a serious threat to Americans' financial lives."

But on June 1, the company announced it was caving. The nation's largest brokerage firm, anchored in tradition and flush with costly full-service brokers, said it was going to enter the world of self-service online stock trading. Merrill's customers, who under the old model could pay brokers commissions of up to several hundred dollars each time they traded, would at the end of the year be able to trade on the Internet for as little as $29.95 per transaction.

It was an important moment. For centuries, information had

been a discriminatory weapon, allowing those who had it to wield it for power or profit over those who didn't. Even giant corporations were set up as information hierarchies; the executive office was the only part of the organization with complete access to information. Everyone else relied on partial information, and the flow of information went from bottom to top.

In the New Economy, information is still power, but *everyone* has it. The Internet has destroyed the old information hierarchies, allowing horizontal as well as vertical flow. Everyone now has access to everything, and power is much more widely dispersed.

As a result, experts, like those at Merrill Lynch, are finding their expertise devalued. In the old world, customers came to Merrill and other full-service brokers because they wanted the benefit of the information that only Merrill could supply. In the new world, that information is readily available in a dozen different places. There's no reason to pay Merrill Lynch so much to do what you can easily do yourself.

The lesson Merrill Lynch learned was this: In the New Economy, there are no experts. Or to put it another way, in the New Economy, *everyone* is an expert.

The Wisdom of Fools

For me, the harbinger of this change arrived in the mail in the summer of 1993. It was a strange and unsolicited newsletter that began, cryptically, with a quote from Shakespeare's *As You Like It:*

> *A fool, a fool! I met a fool i' the forest,*
> *A motley fool.*

A cover letter informed me that I was one of the "chosen few" acquaintances of the editors who had been selected to receive the first edition of *The Motley Fool.* The editors' names weren't familiar to me. A footnote to "acquaintance" clarified: "or an acquaintance of an acquaintance."

The publication was dedicated, the cover letter said, to "energetic writing on *any* subject, in *any* genre, often exhibiting a contrarian point of view, sense of humor not discouraged." There were three odd articles: one profile of the corporate gadflies John Gilbert and Evelyn Y. Davis, one satirical piece about "student" athletes and the NCAA, and one rant about driving through Boston's Callahan tunnel. Then there was an odd exchange of letters with the novelist Julian Barnes, in which the editors attempted to entice him to write a six-sentence short story for their new publication and he declined.

"Nice try . . . but I'm afraid my ideas don't come in response to other people's challenges, but to my own," Barnes had scribbled on a postcard.

And at the end, there was a section on investing.

"The editors are in agreement that the best way to make money over time is the stock market," it said, "not bonds, not gold, not Impressionist art, or baseball cards." Moreover, the mission of the editors was this: to help people invest *on their own.* No need to rely on investment professionals, who get paid by selling you more and more, whether you need it or not. No need for mutual funds, which seldom beat the market anyway. Their goal was a democratic market, cutting out the middleman.

I later learned that the founder of this irreverent jumble, David Gardner, had followed me by a decade as a Morehead Scholar (a program endowed by John *Motley* Morehead, providing another

inspiration for the newsletter's name) at the University of North Carolina. His father was a banking lawyer and had begun talking to his two sons, David and Tom, about investing when they were young boys. "He got across to us the notion that you could become part owners of giant companies," says Gardner. "He'd say 'Hey kids, this chocolate pudding—we *own* that company.' "

When the boys turned eighteen, their father gave each some money, an early inheritance, and told them to invest it on their own. That gave them great freedom, and David took full advantage. After graduating from North Carolina in 1988, he spent four years living in the university town of Charlottesville, Virginia, waiting for his wife, Margaret, to finish school and not doing much of anything else except traveling and occasional freelance writing. "I was living off the money my dad had given me," he says. "I wasn't proud of it. But I was doing tremendous investment research."

David had interned at Salomon Brothers in New York during one of his summers in college, knew what that was like, and had no desire to go back to Wall Street. So in 1992, he and Margaret moved to Alexandria, Virginia, and he took a job writing for *Louis Rukeyser's Wall Street Week* newsletter. That didn't suit him either; his articles would come back heavily edited, with all the personality and opinion drained, he said. If the article was about the benefits of discount brokers, for instance, David would write fervently in favor of them, but the editors would insist on a section laying out the pitfalls of using discount brokers. After only ten months on the job, David, then twenty-seven, quit and decided to start a newsletter of his own, with the help of his brother Tom, then in graduate school at the University of Montana, and a friend named Eryk Rydholm.

The idea for the newsletter wasn't well focused. But the Gard-

ners knew they wanted to do three things. They wanted to share their belief that anyone could do a good job managing his or her own money—without the help of experts. They wanted their "readers to be our writers"—in short, they wanted to create a network. And they wanted to have fun.

After three free monthly issues, each one begging desperately for subscribers at $48 a month, *The Motley Fool* had signed up only sixty people. The project was going nowhere fast. But then, on a lark, Tom Gardner, who had started using the still fledgling America Online computer service to keep up with sports scores, posted a note on an AOL message board, in violation of AOL's prohibition of commercial appeals. "Hi there," the note said. "We're the Motley Fools. We publish a newsletter . . ."

The next day, David Gardner got three phone calls at his Alexandria home from people who had seen his brother's note. A light went on. By December, *The Motley Fool* had established a home for itself in cyberspace. By February, America Online had called, offering to make a Motley Fool site part of its regular service and to pay the Gardners a portion of the money collected from users of the site.

That April, I got a call from David Gardner, out of the blue. He introduced himself and explained how he and his brother had created an April Fool's hoax to expose the penny stock hypesters who were using the online world—in particular Prodigy's Money Talk site—to pump up small stocks they had invested in. The Gardners created a fictitious hypester, Joey Roman, who talked up a phony stock, Zeigletics, on the nonexistent Halifax Canadian exchange. Zeigletics, Joey Roman boasted online, was taking over the toiletry market in Africa and had "recently sponsored the Sudanese equivalent of the Boston Marathon, with hundreds of fans waving plungers at the finish line." Remarkably, many on Money Talk didn't realize this was a joke; some began to inquire how to trade on the Halifax exchange.

I passed David's tale on to reporter Christi Harlan, who wrote an amusing story on the hoax for the *Journal.* That story, says Kara Swisher in her book *AOL.com,* "put the Gardners on the map." It also helped expose Internet stock frauds. The Gardners believed you could jump into the market without a broker; but they didn't believe you could jump in without commonsense.

In June 1994, the Gardners published the last print version of their newsletter and went totally online. In September, AOL subscribers logged 6,000 hours on the new site; in October, 20,000, giving the Motley Fool an income of about $60,000 a month. The next year, AOL's Ted Leonsis paid $500,000 for a 20 percent stake in the company. The Motley Fool became one of the most popular sites on America Online. In the spring, they had signed their first book contract, for *The Motley Fool Investment Guide. Smart Money* magazine said of the Motley Fool site: "Nothing else like it exists. . . . At the very least The Motley Fool will amuse you and possibly educate you, or even enrich you."

By the end of the decade, other online investment sites were doing better than the Fools in the quest for subscribers and for dollars. But the Gardners were the first to capture the investment climate of the age. Investing wasn't just a game for professionals; it was something that any fool, with a little help, could do, and do well.

David and Tom Gardner were prophets of the New Economy. They taught that the experts no longer had a monopoly on information. With remarkably little effort, anyone can have access to all the information the experts have. And by following some fairly simple rules, you probably can handle your own investments even better than they do.

Dow Whatever

In the history of capitalism—in the history of the *world*—there has never been anything quite like the remarkable surge in the U.S. stock market that occurred in the last decade.

No one would have predicted it as the decade began. On New Year's Eve 1990, the Dow Jones industrial average closed at 2633. That number represented the gradual accumulation of industrial might over the course of a century of American history—considered the best years of the mightiest economic power of modern times. It reflected an array of unimagined technological achievements: the dissemination of electricity, the telephone, the television, the computer.

But as 1991 began, the nation was pessimistic. The economy was in recession. In the Murray household, where a baby girl was still learning to sleep through the night, the television was tuned to CNN around the clock, as half a million American troops gathered on the borders of Kuwait, preparing for war. Many American leaders, many leading thinkers, were convinced the American century was over. The next century had already been named: the Asian century.

Two weeks later General Norman Schwarzkopf marched into Kuwait, and the Dow Jones average started to march as well. Over the next nine years, it matched its ninety-six-year total not once, not twice, but three times. And when the Dow finally stopped rising, the NASDAQ market took off. By the end of the decade, the stock market had become the soaring symbol of American rebirth.

American markets accounted for more than half of the world's total market value, up from 29 percent in 1988. The people who had flocked to Japan to learn the secrets of their corporations had spilled back across the Pacific, to Silicon Valley, to study the roots of America's amazingly energetic capitalism.

Rocketing new stars in the market constellation made instant millionaires out of many—even ordinary folk, like those who had the foresight to put a few thousand of their savings into America Online in 1994. Men like Jeff Bezos of Amazon.com, Jay Walker of Priceline.com, and Michael Dell of Dell Computer joined the ranks of the world's billionaires literally overnight, taking their places alongside Warren Buffett and the Sultan of Brunei.

And perhaps most remarkable of all was the spread of the stock market's benefits into ever more American households. A proliferation of 401(k) plans and similar investment vehicles meant stocks accounted for 25 percent of all household assets by the end of the century, up from just 8 percent as recently as 1984. The Dow was still a symbol of the elite; many American families had no part in the market. But by the end of the century nearly half of American households owned some stock, and they were all applauding the market's phenomenal ascent.

As Washington bureau chief of *The Wall Street Journal,* my opportunities to participate in that remarkable market ride have been limited. I couldn't, and wouldn't, buy stock in any company that had interests the Washington bureau might write about. And what big company *didn't* have something at stake in Washington? Tobacco was certainly out. So were pharmaceutical companies, which live or die by decisions of the Food and Drug Administration. So, too, were telecommunications companies, which had much at stake in the decisions of the Federal Communications Commission. I couldn't own Microsoft—we were closely covering the company's struggles with the Department of Justice. And I couldn't own America Online, which had come to the government seeking help in prying open the cable monopolies.

I did have one good investment notion, early in the decade. It was in January of 1991. Looking at post–World War II American history, I had noted that the stock market took a sharp turn northward roughly six months into each previous recession. And the recession we were then in was about six months old. So I called my Merrill Lynch broker and suggested he move all my cash into mutual funds. He resisted. It's too early, he said. There are still big problems out there. He was the expert, and I deferred. On January 17, the Dow Jones industrial average rose 4.6 percent in one day, as the allied attack was launched. By mid-April, with a victory in hand, it crossed the 3000 mark.

My wife and I took our daughter to the victory parade down Pennsylvania Avenue when the war ended. Lucyann waved an American flag as the soldiers marched by. We felt better about America. But we had missed the liftoff of the greatest bull market in world history.

I had another, less fortunate, investment notion in 1997. Part of our job in the Washington bureau of the *Journal* was to keep a close eye on the towering twin figures of the 1990s economy—Federal Reserve Board chairman Alan Greenspan and Treasury secretary Robert Rubin. I followed their on-the-record speeches and statements closely and was treated to some off-the-record embellishment as well. There was no mistaking the fact that both these wise men were very skeptical about the stock market's rise. Greenspan had talked publicly about "irrational exuberance" when the Dow was still under 7000.

So when the Dow hit 8000 that year, I took action: This time, I didn't call my Merrill Lynch broker. But I did call Fidelity, which managed the *Wall Street Journal* profit sharing account. Under profit sharing, I could move my money among funds without tax consequences. I told Fidelity to take all my money out of the market and put it into a money market account. "We'll hit 7000 before we hit 9000," I told friends, "and when we do, I'll go back in." The market never went back.

Doing It Yourself

So why should you take investment advice from me?

Well, that's exactly the point: You shouldn't. Not from me, not from a Merrill Lynch broker, not even from Alan Greenspan or Bob Rubin. In the New Economy, the decision is yours, and yours alone.

Scary? Not really. If you follow some basic guidelines that history has proven to be valuable and avoid some common pitfalls, you'll probably do fine. With very little effort, you can certainly at least match the market's rise—putting you ahead of many mutual fund investors. And you may do even better.

If you've made it to this point in the book, you know step one: Get on the Internet. In managing even the simplest investment portfolio, it's become an essential tool.

Step two: Sign up with an online discount brokerage house. I use Charles Schwab, found online at Schwab.com. That's not because they're the cheapest; they aren't. Other services, like E*Trade, Datek, and Ameritrade will charge you a lower fixed cost per trade. But if you follow the suggestions below, you won't be trading that much anyway—this chapter is about the wisdom of long-term investing, not erratic day-trading. And Schwab is the easiest of the online sites to understand and use, and has a wide range of services.

Step three: Get used to using *independent* sources of information. Discount brokers like Schwab don't have the same web of conflicts of interest that entangles full-service brokers, who get paid commissions on each trade and who are sometimes under pressure to sell particular products. But there are still conflicts. For one thing, Schwab makes its money when you trade. That gives Schwab an incentive to encourage you to trade more than you probably should. For another, it has funds of its own that it wants you to buy.

There are now lots of places to go for independent investment information. But for simplicity's sake, I'd recommend two: SmartMoney.com and the Motley Fool (fool.com) Both sites are free. Both sites are first rate. And they serve somewhat different purposes. SmartMoney is the place to go for serious news and research on individual stocks and mutual funds. I have my own conflict of interest when it comes to SmartMoney, since my employer owns a half interest and I coauthor a monthly column for the magazine. But you can compare it to any other site and I think you'll agree: It has the best investment information, has the best tools for analyzing your investments, and is the easiest to use of any of the investment websites. Motley Fool is more useful for sorting out investment strategies and if you care to, for communicating with other investors.

Most important, both SmartMoney and Motley Fool are scrupulous about maintaining their independence. Neither of them sells investment products or has long-term relationships with brokerage houses. The Gardner brothers go so far as to tell you their investment picks *before* they buy them, so you can get in before they do and so there is no danger of being accused of using their service to pump up the value of their own investments.

If you're really a novice at this, I'd recommend you start by going back to school: SmartMoney University at SmartMoney.com. It won't take you long to read through the coursework, and the education won't cost a penny. But it will provide you a primer on investing, introduce you to key concepts and measurements of value, and then show you how to evaluate both individual stocks and mutual funds you may want to buy.

Now for five basic guidelines. You can choose to ignore them if you wish, but do so at your own risk.

1. Don't put your investment strategy into someone else's hands

The big investment story of the last quarter of the twentieth century has been mutual funds; there are now $5.5 trillion in such funds, up from less than $300 billion in 1982.

But don't follow that crowd. The truth is, many managed mutual funds can't even match the average returns of the market. In 1998, for instance, only 12 percent of all domestic equity funds had returns that beat the Standard & Poor's 500 index, a broad measure of the market. In 1999, the record of mutual fund managers improved, but still more than a third significantly underperformed. But most still lost to the averages. In his 1999 book *Market Shock,* the economist Todd Buchholz points out that over the previous five years, you would have made far more money investing in the stocks of mutual fund companies than investing in mutual funds themselves.

There are reasons for this. One is that you are paying someone a lot of money to manage the fund, and that money gets subtracted from your return. In actively traded funds—and many mutual funds are too actively traded—the trading fees and taxes mount as well. Moreover, big mutual funds are often just too big and clumsy to get the big kick that can sometimes come from investing in successful smaller companies.

There are still times when investing in a mutual fund makes sense. I'll talk below about the value of buying index funds, which track the market indexes. Those tend to have relatively low fees, and if you want to minimize your own effort, they're a good way to go. I also invest in mutual funds to avoid the potential conflicts of interest that come from owning individual stocks.

If you do buy mutual funds, make sure to pick a no-load fund—that means one with no up-front charges, which are often used to pay commissions to full-service brokers. Schwab maintains a long list of no-load funds. Pay attention as well to the funds' overall expenses. Low expenses—well under one percent—not only mean the fund is shaving off less of your return, but also tend to be a pretty good indicator of investment performance. A fascinating study by Morningstar Inc., the Chicago mutual fund research firm, found that funds with low expenses tended to have higher investment returns than those with high expenses—and the difference was much greater than could be accounted for by the expenses themselves!

"Costs are the most powerful determinant of fund performance within category," Morningstar research director John Rekenthaler told my *Journal* colleague Jonathan Clements. "There are no other criteria you could specify that will give you as clear a pattern as this."

While we're on the subject of letting other people make your investment decisions, it's worth pointing out that investment clubs, though popular, usually don't beat the market either. The Beardstown Ladies got a best-selling book out of their boast of a ten-year average return of 23.4 percent, well above the S&P 500's gain of 14.9 percent annually. But an independent audit found the ladies had made a mistake; in fact, the portfolio gained a market-lagging 9.15 percent annually.

Terrance Odean and Brad M. Barber, finance professors at the Graduate School of Management at the University of California, Davis, studied the trading records of 166 clubs that do business with a big discount broker and found that between February 1991 and January 1997, they earned just 14.1 percent. That was nearly 4 percentage points lower than the market index and more than two percentage points less than the typical individual investor. One reason for the poor performance: social dynamics. Clubs often end up buying a stock because they don't want to disappoint the member who did the research.

2. Don't assume the future will be like the recent past

It probably won't. And this is where things get tricky.

The phenomenal market performance of the past decade is luring ever more people into stocks. That may be a good thing, or it may not. It's entirely possible that if you go in now, you're buying at a market top.

The New Economy is for real. Technology, deregulation, globalization, corporate restructuring, and a reinvigoration of markets have created an economic renaissance that will give a powerful prod to growth in the decade ahead. But that doesn't mean stocks will rise at such a steep trajectory forever. People continue to make the same mistakes they always have, assuming that when times have been good, they'll continue to get better. Sooner or later, "irrational exuberance" will set in; maybe it has already. Once it does, the bubble will inevitably burst. Over the long haul, the market will go up. But in the next few years, who knows?

So what should you do? Sit on your hands and wait for the inevitable correction? I tried that and missed 2000 points on the Dow. Now I'm a believer. As the experts will tell you, trying to guess when the market will go up and when it will go down is a fool's game and not a good way to manage your investments. The market will go up and down; but the odds of your figuring out when that's going to happen aren't much better than guessing whether a coin will fall heads or tails.

So take the long view. Over time, the stock market will provide better returns than any other investment. In the short term, you may go through dry spells. The 1930s were a lost decade for investors; if you bought stock on the eve of the 1929 crash, it took nearly two decades to recoup. Same with the 1970s; the Dow flirted with 1000 in early 1966 but didn't permanently break through until 1982.

But even then, if you hung on, the market turned around. Jeffrey Schwartz, a senior consultant at Ibbotson Associates, looked at the market history since World War II and, after throwing out the most extremes examples, found that the longer you held on to your investments, the more reliable the return was. Five-year returns varied from 2.5 percent a year to 22.7 percent; ten-year returns only varied from 4 percent to 20.4 percent; and twenty-year returns ranged from six percent to 15.8 percent. Even in Schwartz's worst-case scenario, if you stayed in for two decades, you would do as well in the stock market as you would in Treasury bonds.

Some optimists argue that in today's market, you'll do much better than that. Glassman and Hassett's *Dow 36,000* was published and edited, like this one, by John Mahaney at Random House. That book makes an intriguing argument for why stocks remain undervalued and still have a long way upwards to go. My guess is the book will someday end up on the shelves next to Ravi Batra's *The Great Depression* of 1990. But who knows?

I certainly don't.

3. To make money, you have to save money

The toughest part of accumulating wealth is saving. Whether you get a 5 percent or a 10 percent return on your money is ultimately less important than whether you are adding regularly to your pool of capital.

In their book *The Millionaire Next Door*, Thomas Stanley and William Danko show that the average millionaire is not someone who got rich taking an Internet firm public and not someone who drives a Mercedes Benz, wears an expensive watch, and has a big swimming pool in the backyard. The average millionaire is someone of relatively modest means who has had the discipline to consistently spend less than he or she has earned.

One tool that can help you do this yourself is personal finance software like Quicken. I use Quicken to track all of our family spending and to match it monthly against a budget. It's a good way to make sure we're saving what we ought to be.

If you're curious how much you "ought" to be saving, check out SmartMoney.com's retirement savings calculator, which can help you figure out how much you need to meet your retirement goals.

SmartMoney.com also has a college planning guide, which can help you prepare for the cost of your children's education.

4. Don't trade too much; and sell your losers, not your winners

Forget everything you've heard about day-trading. That's for people who have nothing else to do with their lives, and even they often get clobbered. The vast majority of investors trade too much—in part because they are pushed to do so by commission-hungry brokers. The average investor held stocks just eight months in 1999, up from two years a decade ago. But the best strategy is still to buy and hold. That can save you lots of money in commissions; and more important, it keeps you from prematurely dumping good stocks.

When it does come time to sell, remember this: Sell your losing stocks, not your winners.

Professor Odean did a study of stock-market trading for ten thousand discount-brokerage accounts over a seven-year period, and found that winning stock positions were 50 percent more likely to be sold than losing positions. Why? Human nature, I suppose; people like to lock in their gains, but want to avoid taking losses. They cling to the belief the bad things will get better; they hope for happy endings.

That's a mistake. For one thing, loss aversion leads to bad investment decisions. Professor Odean found that over the following year, the winners that investors sold outperformed the losers they retained by 3.4 percent. For another, there are taxes to consider. If you sell a losing stock, you can use the resulting capital loss to offset other capital gains and even shelter some ordinary income. But if you sell a winner, you have to pay the capital gains tax. Hold on to your winners, and you can defer taxes indefinitely.

5. Diversify

As your grandmother put it: Don't put all your eggs in the same basket. This is the oldest and surest investment advice around, yet it's still remarkable how many people fail to follow it. As a result of stock option and incentive programs, for instance, many Americans have way too much of their portfolio invested in their employers' stock. Others invest *only* in high-flying technology stocks.

That's a dangerous route.

The issue here isn't just a trade-off between risk and reward. By diversifying, you certainly can reduce your risk. But there's endless research showing that you can also improve the terms of the risk-reward trade-off. Even if you want to be bold and go for the highest returns possible, you'll still improve your odds by diversifying.

The key to diversifying is finding assets whose values move independently from one another. If you own both Dell Computer and IBM, you'll suffer from a sudden downturn in the personal computer market. But if you own Coca-Cola instead of IBM, you'll be better protected; Coke sales are unlikely to be influenced by the drop in computer sales.

Diversification becomes even more important when buying smaller company stocks. If you think Internet stocks are hot, don't buy one, buy several, so you won't lose all your money if one company goes under. And don't put all your small-company investments in the same industry. Even if Internet stocks seem irresistibly hot, put some of your money in biotech stocks, or nontech stocks, to keep your portfolio balanced.

Building a Portfolio

Those are the basics. Now it's time to start building a portfolio.

The first question to ask yourself is this: "How much money can I afford to put in the stock market?" That will depend on answers to two other questions: "How soon will I need this money?" and "How confident am I in the strength of this economy and this market?" I know I said you shouldn't try to time the market. But you should pay attention to the world around you, sort out whether you think we're on the verge of a depression or at the start of an economic renaissance, and make that a part of your investment decision.

If you are in your thirties and saving for retirement, and you feel the markets and the economy are in solid shape, you'll want to put most of your money in stocks and leave only a small amount—15 to 20 percent—in a money market account or in bonds. (Here, we are talking about government bonds and highly-rated corporate bonds, not junk bonds, which really act more like stocks.)

On the other hand, if you're five years from retirement and worried about the market, you may choose to put a much smaller amount—maybe only 40 percent of your savings—in stocks and keep the majority in less risky investments.

SmartMoney.com has a neat asset allocator that will help you sort this out. You can put in your age and your general level of confidence in the economy, and the allocator will suggest how much you should keep in cash and bonds, and how much you should put in stocks. A good investment vehicle for the money you decide to keep out of the market is the Treasury's inflation-indexed bond. It gives you a guaranteed return, over-and-above inflation, that will protect you from a 1970s-style erosion of your assets.

Once you've made your decision about how much to put into the stock market, you face another critical question: "Do I want to make this as simple as possible, and content myself with returns that match the market? Or do I want to spend a little time managing my investments, and try to beat the market—recognizing, of course, that I might fail?"

These aren't mutually exclusive options; you can try some of both. But let's take them one at a time.

Option 1: Let's make this easy, and match the market

If you choose the first option, the rest is simple: Buy low-cost stock index funds, and hang on to them. You can buy one that tracks the S&P 500, which includes the largest companies in the market; or you can broaden your portfolio even further by buying a fund that tracks the Wilshire 5000, which despite its name includes more than seven thousand stocks, many of them relatively small. Some experts recommend the Wilshire 5000 index funds over the more popular S&P 500 index funds because in certain years, small stocks do better than large. If you just want to buy the biggest, you can get an index fund that tracks the thirty big companies in the Dow Jones industrial average.

My *Journal* colleague Greg Ip, whom I consider one of the sharpest observers of equity markets, says that given the difficulty even the most talented money managers have beating the market, index funds are the *only* way to go. His all-purpose investment strategy: "Subtract your age from the number 80 and put that percentage of your savings in a stock index fund. Put the rest in medium-term Treasury bonds. Then go play golf."

Option 2: Let's try to beat the market; it sounds like fun

Now it's stock-picking time. If you've played with the Smart Money.com asset allocator, you'll notice it recommends that you divide your stock market money among three categories: large caps, small caps, and foreign stocks. Large caps are the big companies that make up the S&P 500 and have total market values—defined as all the shares outstanding multiplied by the price per share—of $5 billion or more. Small caps can have market values of anywhere from $250 million to $5 billion and tend to be much riskier investments.

If you are young and open to risk, the asset allocator will suggest you put a bigger chunk of your money into small caps; even though they are riskier stocks, they offer you a chance at bigger returns. If you are nearing retirement, it'll suggest you put more into the big, safe, large-cap companies.

Let's take these three categories, one at a time, starting with foreign stocks.

Foreign Stocks. I seldom disagree with the smart folk at Smart-Money, but here's one place where I do. The truth is, you don't need foreign stocks in your portfolio. The idea is to give you diversity, which as noted above, is a good principle. There will be times when the U.S. market is weak and foreign markets are strong, and owning foreign stocks will help your return.

But in the New Economy, it's no longer necessary to own foreign stocks to go global. American companies can and will take you overseas. The thirty companies in the Dow industrials now get on average 40 percent of their sales overseas. Chrysler is now Daimler-Chrysler AG, based in Germany, and still trades on the New York

Stock Exchange. Amoco Corp. is now BP Amoco PLC, based in Britain, but also available on the New York Stock Exchange. Ford purchased Volvo's car operations and is one of Europe's biggest carmakers. Even regional companies are going global. Texas Utilities Co. purchased utilities in Australia and Britain; Baby Bell Ameritech purchased 20 percent of Bell Canada.

The result: American investors can get the benefits of overseas diversification without leaving home. In a story that ran in April 1999, Greg Ip quoted Tom McManus, an equity strategist at NationsBanc Montgomery Securities. "Some investors have traveled the world to try to understand the customs and sociology of companies around the world," said McManus, "but you're still stuck with currency problems, accounting differences and, in many cases, different classes of stock." A good U.S. multinational, on the other hand, "is the best of all possible worlds," McManus says. You get the diversification that comes from investing overseas, but with it, "we've got New York Stock Exchange liquidity, we've got Securities and Exchange Commission transparency, we've got conference calls in English, and we have American can-do management."

If you think you know enough to make a good overseas stock choice, go ahead and do it. But don't be bullied by conventional wisdom into thinking you have to invest overseas. When choosing large-cap stocks, just make sure you pick some that have a heavy presence in other markets, for diversity's sake.

Large-cap stocks. This is where the game starts to get tricky. You want some big stocks for your portfolio; but how to choose? Some experts will tell you to go for value; others tell you to go for growth.

The idea behind value investing is finding stocks that have relatively low prices and thus are bargains. The problem here is that when a stock has a relatively low price, it's often for good reason. In that first *Motley Fool* newsletter, the Gardners' large-cap stock pick was F.W. Woolworth Co. The reason: It was cheap. "The company's stock has been such a woofer for so long that its $1.16 annual dividend looks juicy," the Fools wrote. At a market price of 27 1/8 ($27.125), the stock had a high "yield" of 4.3 percent.

In fact, Woolworth woofed because it was a dog. The company later changed its name to Venator, but that did little to help. By the end of the decade, as the market roared, Venator fizzled to $10 a share.

Value investors have a particular problem in today's market; by historical measures, there appear to be no bargains. So-called P/E ratios—the ratio of a company's stock price to its earnings per share—are higher than ever, far higher than analysts used to think possible or desirable.

Growth investors, on the other hand, look for the standouts, the companies that are delivering big increases in profits, year after year: General Electric, Cisco Systems, Microsoft. These investors understandably want the very best of American business. Problem is, so does everyone else. Growth companies tend to have high prices; how much higher can they go?

One recently popular measure that attempts to account for both value and growth is called the PEG ratio. It is calculated by dividing the company's P/E ratio by the company's expected annual growth rate for the coming years.

For instance, suppose IBM is trading at $60 a share, and has earnings of $3 a share. Its P/E ratio is thus 20 (60/3). If analysts are predicting earnings growth of about 10 percent a year for the next few years, that would mean a PEG ration of 2 (20/10).

Conventional wisdom holds that a fairly priced stock should have a PEG ratio of 1. But there's little intellectual justification for this approach—or, for that matter, for most investment strategies. And these days, trying to find a stock with a PEG ratio of less than 1 won't get you far; that bargain basement has long since closed. (By the way, don't worry about the math here; SmartMoney.com will calculate both P/E and PEG ratios for you.)

Motley Fool offers a guide to putting together what he calls a "Rule Maker" portfolio—ten great companies that you can hold for ten years and that will outperform the market. The goal here is not so much to look for bargains, but to look for the corporate right stuff and then to buy and sit tight. His original list, put together in 1995, included companies like Dell Computer, America Online, Gap, Cisco Systems, Microsoft, Sun Microsystems, and Intel—all huge winners. It also included two companies that didn't do as well—Texas Instruments and Hewlett-Packard—and one real dog, Silicon Graphics.

With a portfolio like that, you could sleep well at night.

Small-cap stocks. Do you love risk? Do you want to make really big money? Are you still kicking yourself over the fact that you didn't buy America Online in 1992? (Or for that matter in 1993 or 1994 or 1995 or 1996?) Then the small-cap stocks are the place for you.

But be careful; this isn't a game for weak stomachs. If you invest in General Electric, there's little chance you'll lose your shirt. But if you invest in one of these guys, you might. This needs to be money you can afford to miss. Remember, America Online was dogged for years by predictions it would be driven under once Americans discovered they didn't have to pay to get on the Internet. Those predictions could have proven true.

Just because these stocks are risky, that doesn't mean you shouldn't research them thoroughly. Don't make investments based on a tip heard in a bar. Do your homework. And try to invest in what you know. If you have expertise in a particular industry, try picking stocks in that industry. If a company's making a product you really like, look into that company. You're likely to do better if you invest in things you know.

The Gardners also offer some tips for putting together what they call a "Rule Breaker" portfolio. This is an aggressive portfolio that embraces risk, ignores traditional measures of valuation, and seeks the highest possible return. The idea here is to look for companies that are about to take off.

Another popular approach these days, laid out in the book *The Gorilla Game,* by Geoffrey A. Moore, is to attempt to identify the companies that will benefit from discontinuous innovation in the future. These companies are the ones that may become the next Microsoft or the next Cisco—that will set a new technological standard and be able to reap the benefits of that standard for years afterward. This is an incredibly ambitious strategy, but one that's tailored to the remarkable changes of our times. The authors of the book have set up a website, gorillagame.com, for those who want to join the hunt.

I took a stab at this in August 1999 and bought 200 shares of a northern Virginia company called MicroStrategy, whose chief executive, Michael Saylor, I had met earlier in the year. The company specializes in data mining—digging into enormous databases to find useful information—and seemed to be at the forefront of the next wave of Internet businesses. Within the next seven months, those shares had risen as high as $600—a return of 2,000 percent!

Don't let your search for high-tech superstars focus on electronic technology alone; the biomedical world is on the verge of a revolution as well. That could turn out to be where the best buys are.

Keep in mind, though, that the hottest technology companies can quickly turn cold. Consider the fate of Pointcast, which was going to revolutionize the Internet by pushing information onto your screen overnight, or Iridium, which was going to revolutionize communications with a cell phone you could use anywhere. Pointcast crumbled before it could go public, and was taken over; Iridium went bankrupt, leaving investors out of luck.

Remember also that the danger in any hot stock-picking strategy is that once it becomes too hot, it can stop working, as a flood of investor acolytes push up prices of the chosen stocks until they are no longer a bargain.

That's the frustrating thing about trying to beat the market. You've got to keep ahead of the conventional wisdom, not fall behind it.

Good luck! And for safety's sake, keep a big piece of your money in large-cap stocks or, even better, in index funds. Odds are high that you'll discover you can't beat the market either. But at least you can have some fun trying.

10

Starting a
Business in the
New Economy

Ideas Will Make You Rich

Follow money throughout history, and you can see how the sources of wealth have changed. For most of the last millennium, when food was scarce, land was the key, providing wealth to those who owned it. Later, as the Industrial Revolution exploded, energy became the critical factor, enabling John D. Rockefeller to accumulate previously unimagined personal wealth by cornering the oil market. As capitalism matured, wealth accrued to the capitalists—the people and giant global companies who had money to begin with and could put that money to work making things.

But today, more than ever before in human history, wealth follows people and ideas. To become wealthy in the New Economy, it's not necessary to conquer vast lands, to control huge oil reserves, to build vast factories for mass production, or to have access to large amounts of capital. It's only necessary to have the right idea. Money follows.

Get Rich, Click

I learned that lesson one night over a lavish dinner at Galileo, Washington's premier Italian restaurant. Seated around the table, as we dined on a tasting meal of octopus salad, risotto with quail, and veal with truffles, were the elite entrepreneurs of northern Virginia's burgeoning high-tech world. Among them were Jim Kimsey, a founder of America Online; Raj Singh, founder of LCC International; Mark Warner, cofounder of Nextel; Russ Ramsey of the investment Bank Friedman, Billings and Ramsey; and Michael Saylor, the thirty-six-year-old billionaire who runs MicroStrategy.

The group, called Capital Investors Inc., had joined forces and pooled some money for the purpose of encouraging start-ups in northern Virginia. And after their sumptuous meal on this evening, they heard from a thirty-year-old woman named Angie Kim and her two partners, who wanted their help.

Angie Kim was born in Korea and moved to Baltimore at age thirteen. She had never run a business before, although she had helped her immigrant parents run several stores. At the time of the dinner, she had no customers, no revenues, no assets to speak of, and only eight employees. She and her partners were designing a website, but it wasn't up and running yet.

But she had a stellar résumé: highest honors and Phi Beta Kappa from Stanford, magna cum laude at Harvard Law School, editor of the *Law Review*.

And she had an idea. She wanted to start a business called

EqualFooting.com. It would help small businesses combine forces over the Internet to purchase needed goods and services, giving them the same kind of buying clout that big companies have. Her plan was to grow the company to encompass a quarter-million small-business customers by the end of the year 2000.

The most startling part of Ms. Kim's presentation was this: She was out to raise $6 million from investors, who in return would get just one-third of the ownership of the company. She and her partners would keep the other two-thirds. To put it another way, this young Korean-American woman and her partners were boldly trying to convince a roomful of seasoned and successful entrepreneurs that they and their idea were worth $12 million. That was their initial, or "pre-money," valuation of the two-thirds ownership of the company they planned to keep for themselves.

After Ms. Kim left the room, the entrepreneurs discussed the idea. One complained it was too diffuse—exactly what kind of small-business customers did she intend to cultivate? Others worried about the management teams' lack of hands-on experience. But in the end, the group agreed to fund the young woman, giving her a big boost on the path to Internet success.

Venture capital, of course, is as old as capitalism itself. There have always been people with money willing and eager to back a promising new business.

But what's changed in recent years is this: In the past, those who provided the money ended up owning most of the business. As recently as a decade ago, "80–20" deals were the rule—80 percent of the business went to the venture capitalist, and 20 percent to the entrepreneur. Today that's changed. The venture capitalists will often take as little as 30 or 40 percent and leave the entrepreneur with the rest. Power has shifted from the people with the money to the person with the idea.

Some of this may be simple supply and demand; too much venture capital money chasing too few good ideas. But I think there's more to it than that. With the economy crossing new frontiers of technology, and with information at the center of it all, ideas are worth more than they used to be. In a knowledge economy, good ideas are the mother lode.

I've seen this New Economy take hold through the eyes of my friend and college roommate, Tom Darden, who made his first fortune in a quintessential old economy endeavor—the brick business. Today, he lives in Raleigh, North Carolina, and uses the money he has accumulated to provide venture capital to the businesses of the future. A look at the businesses he's funded provides a road map to the sources of wealth in the New Economy.

Take the case of Holden Thorp, a thirty-four-year-old chemist from Fayetteville, North Carolina. Thorp got excited by a high school chemistry course, studied chemistry at the California Institute of Technology, did postgraduate work at Yale, and then settled back as a professor at the University of North Carolina. He dreamed of science, not riches. He would have been content to spend his days studying how DNA gets altered within cells and how that leads to aging, cancer, and other biological changes. He wanted his work to be on the cutting edge of science, but never expected it to earn him a fortune. Like most academic chemists, he thought his life would consist of getting grants from the government, doing research, and then writing papers about it.

But in the fall of 1994, Thorp found a man his own age sitting in the front row of his freshman chemistry lecture. The man had been an entrepreneur but had returned to school to learn more about biotechnology. He showed Thorp a story in *The Wall Street Journal* about a company in California called Affymetrix. The company was doing DNA research similar to Thorp's and had figured out how to put millions of human gene particles on a half-inch silicon chip. Affymetrix was now preparing to market those chips as a cheap and easy way of diagnosing cystic fibrosis, certain types of cancer, and drug resistance in AIDS patients, and even as a way of settling questions of paternity.

The article opened up a whole new world to Thorp. Through his own research, he had found a potentially cheap and easy way to determine the presence of a gene and to explore how that gene responds to various chemicals. He began to realize his technique might make the search for new genetic drugs much faster and easier than it is now. He knew nothing about business. But he hooked up with a group of venture capitalists, including Tom Darden, who helped him find the people he needed to run one.

Starting in December 1996, Darden and others began providing funding to the new company, Xanthon, pouring in nearly $10 million over three years. Before even taking his product to market, Thorp had become a paper millionaire. If his product succeeds, he'll be that many times over.

The opportunity for a smart, academically minded chemist to make millions is one that neither he nor his university colleagues would have dreamed of a decade ago. Even now, Thorp says, "I don't have any interest in leaving academia. I'm not interested in the management aspects. I like doing research and working with students."

But Thorp's experience is becoming increasingly common.

Academia generates ideas; ideas generate wealth. Schools like MIT and Stanford have become hotbeds for entrepreneurs; the staff of the MIT computer lab, for instance, has a combined personal net worth estimated to be $1 billion or more.

Not all good ideas come from academia, of course. Todd Huvard is no academic. He is a small-time publisher and airplane enthusiast. But now he's working with Darden and a couple of other venture capitalists on a plan to start an Internet business. Huvard started out his career as a journalist, writing stories for the tiny *Tidewater Review.* But he quickly found that on $170 a week, he could barely live, much less pursue his hobby of flying. So he went into business, migrating from insurance to making sand-blasted redwood signs, and finally, in 1987, to running a magazine for private airplane pilots.

Huvard's real break came in 1995, when he stumbled onto the Internet. By April of that year, he had started up his website. Soon thereafter, he began a business helping others design websites. "The Internet then was like the Wild West," he says. He specialized in aviation websites and designed a site for the Aircraft Owners & Pilots Association, among others.

The idea that got the attention of the venture capitalists was his plan to create online "virtual" catalogs for companies that have a line of products to sell but don't have the time or expertise to create their own Internet catalogs. As Huvard sees it, his company will be the ultimate intermediary. He'll bring customers to a business by arranging links to that business's catalogs from other, related websites and offering a commission to the people who run those referring websites for each item sold as a result of the link. He'll design the online catalogs, and he'll handle the orders. But unlike, say,

Amazon.com, he won't have to keep any inventory. His venture capital buddies think it's a great idea and expect it to grow into a $100 million business in three years.

"Today there are just more opportunities for people like me who have ideas, but need capital," he says. "Instead of having to jump through hoops for bankers—guys who have never had to take a risk—I can talk to venture capital guys who understand business and understand there's a chance it won't work out."

Tom Darden's own career in business illustrates how profound the changes in American capitalism have been in the last two decades. Like so many of his generation, he began adulthood with vaguely anticapitalist, even anti-American sentiments. At the University of North Carolina, he studied anthropology and city planning. He dreamed of becoming a government-employed environmental planner.

Tom married a wonderful woman, Jody Ragland, deferred his acceptance to Yale Law School, and went off to Korea on a Luce scholarship. Darden worked on urban waste issues at the Korea Institute of Science and Technology. But while in Asia, he discovered that in comparison to the rest of the world, the United States wasn't such a bad place. More important, he gained a respect for the free enterprise and entrepreneurialism that was lifting Korea out of its post-war rubble. By the time he returned home, the anticapitalist sentiments of his college days were gone, and he was determined to become an entrepreneur.

At Yale, Tom took courses at the business school as well as the law school. He joined Bain and Company, a business-consulting firm that had decided to take on a few law graduates as an experiment. At Bain, he learned to analyze business, and he spent his spare time reading *Inc.* and *Venture* and trying to think of a business he could start on his own.

The opportunity came from his father-in-law, Bill Ragland, who owned Cherokee Brick, in North Carolina, and wanted out. Tom proposed to buy the company. His father-in-law pointed out he was twenty-eight-years-old, had never run a business, and had no money, and suggested that Tom first come to North Carolina and run the business before buying it. But Tom insisted on an outright purchase, not eager to go into business with his father-in-law. Eventually, Ragland agreed.

To make the business sustainable, Darden decided he also needed to buy Sanford Brick Corporation, a larger company headquartered just ten miles away. Sanford Brick was bigger than Cherokee, but troubled. Owned by a company in Texas, it was losing money and was flooding the North Carolina market with low-quality bricks at cheap prices. With remarkable chutzpah, and no money, Darden called the Texas company and offered to buy Sanford. He was invited to Texas to talk.

First Union Bank had agreed to help Darden buy his father-in-law's company, but balked at giving him the additional funds to purchase Sanford because of its size and lack of profitability. Other big banks did the same. His father-in-law also advised against the purchase. But Tom was tenacious, and a small-town bank in Sanford finally agreed to lend him the money he needed, in order to keep the brick company alive. He and some other key managers bought both companies.

Brick-making technology in 1984 was pretty much the same as it had been in 1950. But by going to the plants every day and working closely with the workers, Darden found plenty of ways to improve their efficiency, reducing oil leakage here, saving a step in the manufacturing line there. He also put his interest in environmental issues to work. While expanding one of the plants in 1985, excavators discovered petroleum in the ground that had leaked from storage tanks. Darden called the regulators, who told him to excavate all the contaminated soil and haul it to the local landfill. Instead, Darden proposed mixing polluted clay with his brick-making clay and burning off the oil in the process. The regulators agreed, and Cherokee Environmental Group eventually became the largest remediator of oil-contaminated soil in the mid-Atlantic area.

In 1985, just two years after buying the brick companies, Darden sold them to Jim Walter Corporation for $12 million more than he had paid. He spent only a little of his share of the money, buying a new car for his wife, adding a guest room to his (brick) house, and buying an expensive leather briefcase, which he later gave away. The rest of the money became the start of his new business: venture investing.

His first three deals included one in medical products, one in restaurants, and one in real estate. The real estate and restaurant ventures, remnants of the old economy, both failed. He still keeps a copy of the restaurant company's stock certificate on his office wall, to remind him of the failure.

But the medical business became an enormous success, returning thirty times the money he invested. That gave him money for further investments, and soon made Tom Darden a name well known among anyone seeking venture capital in North Carolina's "Research Triangle" area.

Many of the fifty or so investments Darden has been involved in are at or near the leading edge of the New Economy. He continues his interest in environmental problems and runs a $250 million fund called Cherokee Investment Partners II that buys up contaminated property and cleans it. Among its first investments is a large piece of land in Bayonne, New Jersey, that's going to be cleaned up and turned into a golf course, reachable by boat from Manhattan.

By buying and cleaning up land, Tom's convinced he's doing something that's both good for society and good for his fellow investors. Many people who own contaminated land, he's found, are "terrified of regulators and liability" and therefore willing to sell cheap. "I didn't mind the regulators, and I felt that we did not need to fear the liability as long as we cleaned the property up to a level they accepted."

Could You Be Next?

"Everybody's Getting Rich But Me!" read the cover of *Newsweek* magazine, capturing the yuppie angst of our age. America has always had its wealthy. But never before has it had so many, created so quickly, and often living right next door.

The ranks of millionaires in this country are expanding faster than a Mercedes dealer can count. By one estimate, there were three million in 1995, four million in 1998, and who knows how many today. The club of American billionaires would now barely fit into Bill Gates's mansion, with *Forbes* magazine estimating 250 this year, up 60 from last year. The financial markets have gladly fueled the flame, snapping up the initial public stock offerings (IPOs) of fledgling companies in the late 1990s as if they were winning lottery tickets, and creating vast fortunes literally overnight. "Have you done your IPO yet?" has become a greeting of sorts among tech entrepreneurs. "The good news is, you'll be a millionaire soon" blared a recent piece in *Wired* magazine. "The bad news is, so will everybody else."

And the pace shows no sign of letting up. The Internet, still in its infancy, has already spawned "the largest legal creation of wealth ever," says Russ Ramsey, whose northern Virginia investment bank now sells IPOs to investors online.

It's all a little dizzying; even a little discomfiting. But behind all this wealth are stories of human triumph. Entrepreneurs are the key to success in the New Economy and the key to America's resurgence. According to one recent study, as many as one in twelve Americans are trying to start their own business—far more than in any other industrialized nation.

Could you be one of those people? If so, the time has never been better. A revolution in technology is creating business opportunities as never before, and a revolution in finance is making plenty of money available for new entrepreneurs.

The vast majority of all successful businesses start small and never need to seek venture capital funding. They get funded from their own revenues, from bank loans, or from personal resources.

But if you think you have an idea that could grow quickly and needs an infusion of venture capital to be a success, read on. Below are twelve questions, compiled with the help of some of the nation's most successful venture financiers, that will help you know if your idea can go the distance.

Twelve Questions for the Would-Be Entrepreneur

1. Is this idea obvious to others?
If it is, you're probably too late.

2. Are you selling aspirin or vitamins?
Wake up in the middle of the night with a headache, and you'll do anything for an aspirin—even drive to the 24-hour pharmacy. That's the kind of product the venture funds want to finance, something that relieves a pain or fulfills a pressing need. Vitamins may be good for you, but you can, and most likely will, get along just fine without them.

3. Do you know who your customers will be?
Too many business plans take a *Field of Dreams* approach to their future customers: Build it and they will come. To get investors, you'll need to show that you know what your customer base is and you know what it'll take to get those customers on board. Remember, in the New Economy, getting the attention of your customer is often the biggest challenge.

4. Is the market big enough?
Venture capitalists don't aim for modest success. They're looking for the big hit. Many of their deals go bust, many more just plod along; but it's the small handful that make ten to fifty times the initial investment that they live for. That means your business needs to have a shot at growing quickly into a $50 million or $100 million en-

terprise, or they won't be interested. The market for your product or service has to be large; selling bird-shaped lawn ornaments to ornithologists won't cut it.

On the other hand, it's best that the market not be *too* big, or there's a greater risk a well-capitalized player will jump in and squish you like a bug.

5. Is your business scalable?

You won't find "scalable" in the dictionary, but you'll hear it a lot among the entrepreneurial set. The days of building a business brick by brick or store by store are long gone. In today's winner-take-all environment, you need to be able to move quickly from the garage to the global bazaar. You need to show you have a plan for, and understand the demands of, meteoric growth.

6. Can you create an unfair advantage over your competitors?

From the businessman's point of view, competition is a drag. It drives down profit margins. Even the most brilliant idea won't sell if it's an idea that can be quickly and easily copied by others, who may have more money to begin with. From day one, you have to think about how to keep others out; that's how Bill Gates got where he is.

7. Will it be difficult for customers to switch to your product or service?

As discussed in earlier chapters, switching costs are a huge consideration in the networked economy. I might be able to create word processing software that's twice as easy to use as Microsoft Word, but there's little chance I'll be able to get anyone to switch and use it.

Enron badly miscalculated the high cost of getting Californians to switch their electrical providers. Your funders aren't likely to let you make the same mistake.

8. Are you asking for enough money?

One sure way to ruin a good idea is to underfund it. Be realistic in your assessment of the money you need to make your business a success, and ask for that amount.

9. Will you ever make money?

Maybe not today, maybe not tomorrow, but *someday* you've got to have profits. Particularly in the Internet world, too many business plans are based on neat ideas that everyone may want to use but no one wants to pay for. Will this business eventually provide long-term revenues that will exceed expenses—*including* the expense of acquiring customers?

10. Can you explain your idea clearly and simply?

When you tell friends about your idea, how often do they blink in the first thirty seconds? Can you get your business plan into one three-ring binder, rather than two or three? Can you summarize it in ten pages rather than twenty? Can you explain it to a potential sponsor in less than thirty minutes, without having them look at their watch? Your ability to articulate your idea is the first and best test of how well-focused it is.

11. Are you and your business plan flexible enough to adapt to changing circumstances?

To succeed, you need a clear focus. But you can't be set in cement. Your investors are going to be watching to see if you're a good listener, if you can stand criticism of your idea, if you're willing to hire people who are smarter than you are and share power with them. In a rapidly changing world, flexibility is critical.

12. Will your personal life allow you to chase this dream?

Can your marriage survive? Are you prepared to be away from friends and colleagues, and live in solitary confinement with your idea? If your idea works, will you be proud of what you created? Can you pursue this opportunity *and* be true to yourself?

11

Retiring in the New Economy

Old Age Isn't What It Used to Be

Three powerful demographic trends are converging to make aging far more precarious in the New Economy.

The first and most important is a triumph of medicine. When Franklin Roosevelt signed the social security program into law in 1935, the average American wasn't expected to live past 61. Today, the average life expectancy is 76 and climbing. One in three girls born today is likely to live to 90.

Constant advances in medicine are pushing that frontier ever higher. The number of deaths from coronary heart disease has been plummeting, thanks to cholesterol-lowering drugs, more aggressive diagnosis of high blood pressure, and declining tobacco use. Colon cancer, which has been a leading cause of death, is now almost entirely preventable with timely medical examination. The scourge of breast cancer is being dramatically weakened with improved therapies.

So far, this book has dealt mostly with electrical-based technologies. But the advances in medical science have been no less significant. And the biggest revolution lies ahead. The Human Genome Project may help isolate and conquer many hereditary conditions in the coming decades.

Medical advances have so steadily reduced threats to longevity that the most significant things robbing us of long lives in the New Economy are behaviors that are totally within our control. Habits such as smoking and neglecting to use vehicle seatbelts and motorcycle helmets, as well as failure to practice safe sex, to install smoke detectors, and to stay out of the sun, are fast becoming the biggest reasons we're not all living into our nineties.

The second critical trend affecting retirement is demographic. The baby boom generation, the largest and most politically potent generation in American history, is on the eve of its retirement. At each stage of their lives, baby boomers have brought great change to American society; retirement promises to be no different.

To see the future, visit Florida. At the turn of the last century, only one in twenty-five Americans was over the age of 65. At the turn of this one, it's one in eight. Thirty years from now, it will be one in five—the same ratio found in Florida today.

Moreover, in spite of these trends, many people continue to retire early. More than 70 percent of social security beneficiaries begin to collect benefits before age sixty-five. As a result, working Americans are running an economy that has to support an ever-larger burden of retirees. In 1950, there were sixteen active workers for every one retiree; by 2030, the ratio will be just two to one.

And consider this: As one generation enjoys unparalleled longevity, the next has delayed ever later the decision to have children. As a result, many Americans in the New Economy find them-selves faced with three of the greatest financial challenges of life all at once: preparing for their own retirement, putting their children through college, and caring for aged parents.

The third critical trend is the changing nature of work, dis-cussed in Chapter 8. Gone is the paternalistic employer who, in return for a life's work, would provide a healthy pension that al-lowed you to spend your last years comfortably traveling, baby-sitting grandchildren, playing shuffleboard, and winding your gold watch.

Today, fewer than half of all workers are enrolled in an em-ployer-sponsored pension plan. Among small companies—those with twenty-five or fewer employees—only 17 percent of workers have access to a retirement plan at work.

And even those who have generous company plans find those plans have changed from two decades ago. In the old economy, de-fined-benefit plans helped tie an employee to a company for life. Pension benefits were calculated based on your salary at retirement and your years of service. The company assumed all the financial risk and gave you the security.

Today, more benefits reside in defined-contribution plans, in which the company makes a contribution to your retirement each year, but assumes no responsibility for what happens to you or that money after you retire. Bad investment decisions can cause the pen-sion pool to dwindle; so, too, can decisions to tap those resources before retirement.

Even the traditional defined-benefit plans that remain in place are rapidly changing. In the last few years, many large companies have, like IBM, switched their pension plans to a cash balance approach, offering more flexibility to younger workers but less for more experienced workers. Twelve percent of employers offered cash balance plans last year, up from 5 percent in 1995.

All of this has caused more than a little anxiety among Americans eyeing retirement.

A recent AARP survey found that 63 percent of American adults would prefer *not* to live to 100. Fear of failing health was their top reason, followed closely by fear of failing finances.

Three-Legged Stool

The financing for retirement has frequently been referred to as a "three-legged stool," consisting of social security, private pensions, and personal savings. Today, all three legs are rickety. So it's worth taking a look at each.

Social Security

After two decades of political demagoguery over social security, younger Americans are convinced social security won't be there when they retire.

But they are wrong. The truth is, social security is the strongest leg of the stool. And the reason is simple political calculus.

Consider this: In the 1996 election, just under half the electorate aged 25 to 44 turned out to vote; but 67 percent of those aged 65 or over voted. More than half of all voters were over the age of 45.

Now think about what happens as the population ages and every member of Congress has a constituency that looks like St. Petersburg's. Do you think any of them will vote for significant cuts in social security? Not likely.

What about the much-discussed bankruptcy of social security? Well, no question there's a problem. As the population ages, the strain on the social security program will be immense. The latest estimates suggest that starting a decade and a half from now, social security payments to beneficiaries will exceed payroll tax collections from workers. And come 2032, the trust fund will indeed run out of money.

But there are two things to remember about those estimates. The first is they are based on a fairly slow rate of productivity growth, of the sort we got accustomed to in the 1970s and 1980s, but well below the levels of the 1950s and 1960s. If the New Economy delivers faster growth—as many believe it will—the day of reckoning for social security could get pushed back considerably. The key to the social security equation is not how many people are working, but how much they earn in wages and salary. If the New Economy delivers higher earnings, social security payroll tax revenues will increase, and the day of insolvency will be delayed, perhaps even indefinitely.

The second thing to remember is this: Even when the trust fund is exhausted, *nothing happens.* The law still requires benefits to be paid. When the trust fund is exhausted, the government will simply draw down general Treasury funds to pay benefits or, if necessary, borrow.

The Clinton administration has already set the stage for using general revenues to fund social security. It has proposed giving the social security system surplus funds to buy up outstanding general government debt, so that the interest and principal paid on that debt goes into the social security fund, instead of the Treasury.

That's just a backdoor method of using general revenues to prop up social security thirty years from now.

The real danger three decades hence is not that social security goes bust, but that the rest of the government goes begging. As retirees lay claim to more and more of the government's revenues, less will be left to fund roads, law enforcement, children's health, national defense, and just about any other function of government. Services will decline, or taxes will be raised to pay for them. Either way, the economy could suffer. But social security beneficiaries won't.

There could be some significant changes in the program. Support is growing for plans that take a portion of the social security payroll tax and put it in "individual accounts," giving individuals some leeway in determining how the money is invested. There might even be some modest reductions in benefits for future beneficiaries. The retirement age, for instance, already slated to move from 65 to 67, could be pushed up another year or two.

But you can count on this: As long as the United States is a democracy, social security recipients will get their benefits, in one form or another.

Employer Pensions

In an economy that valued experience, pensions were designed to lock you into your job until retirement. The formulas, based on years of service, ensured that the lion's share of retirement benefits were earned in your final few years on the job. If you left early, you got little.

But in the New Economy, where talent trumps experience, those old-style pensions don't suit the interests of employers. They would rather have a plan that lets them compete for younger workers. Often, the old-style pensions don't suit the interests of workers either. They would prefer something more portable, something that lets them move from job to job without sacrificing benefits.

This has led to the rise of 401 (k) plans, in which the worker has to take more of the responsibility for his or her own retirement, and more of the risk. The company makes contributions, but often only to match those the worker makes. Workers have substantial control over how their money is invested; and if they change jobs, they can take their 401 (k) money with them.

Such 401 (k) plans are often a wonderful benefit, and have helped fuel the flood of money into the stock market. The best part of the deal is that the government chips in—contributions to 401(k) plans are usually tax exempt, and their earnings are as well. But here's a surprising fact: *Only 21 percent of the people with 401 (k) plans contribute the maximum amount that their employer will match.* That means corporate pension dollars are left lying on the table. That's foolish.

Here's another surprising fact: Only 40 percent of all the distributions made from such plans when people change jobs are rolled over into other tax-deferred retirement plans. In other words, much of the money is being used by beneficiaries before they reach retirement.

Bottom line: Employer-provided 401 (k) plans provide workers who have them with great opportunities to save for retirement. But many workers aren't taking full advantage of those plans. And many more don't have access to them. The second leg is still surprisingly shaky.

Personal Savings

The answer to the trends cited above is clear enough: People need to save more for retirement. The New Economy not only puts power in your hands, it puts responsibility in your hands. You have to provide for your own future.

Problem is, that's not happening. Household savings in the United States has been abysmally low, and in much of 1999 it was actually negative—the worst since the Great Depression. Despite ever more incentives offered up by Congress, Americans don't save.

This, too, may be a function of American optimism. According to a 1999 survey by the Employee Benefit Research Institute, 69 percent of Americans are at least "somewhat confident" that they're taking the necessary steps to retire comfortably. But only half of those surveyed have ever tried to figure out how much money they'll need to maintain their standard of living in retirement. Two-thirds of the respondents haven't thought about long-term-care insurance, and just 16 percent of the people surveyed have saved more than $100,000 toward their retirement.

The average household headed by someone between 55 and 64 years of age reports a pitiful $28,000 in assets, excluding home equity—far too little to fund twenty or thirty years of retirement, or even one year in a nursing home. Social security will only provide up to $16,500 a year, and yet the Social Security Administration reports that its benefit checks provide the major source of income to 66 percent of beneficiaries and the *only* source of income to 18 percent.

But don't take my word for it. Here's how a recent report from the National Commission on Retirement Policy sponsored by the Center for Strategic and International Studies summed it up:

Quite simply, we—as a country and as individuals—are ill-prepared to meet the financial challenges of the twenty-first century. We are confronted with a rapidly aging population, actuarially unsound federal health and retirement programs, unsustainable trends of spending for government programs for senior citizens, and inadequate levels of private savings. We have promised too much collectively, and set aside too little individually. As a result, the proverbial "three-legged" stool of resources for retirement security—Social Security, private pension plans, and personal savings—that traditionally has financed Americans' retirement is increasingly unstable and in need of repair.

What You Should Do

But enough about what other people aren't doing to prepare for retirement. The question is: What should you do?

The simple answer, of course, is to save. What's offered below is a five-step plan that will help you prepare for the golden decades.

1. Start saving for retirement now, no matter how old you are

Compound interest works miracles if you give it time. A 25-year-old who saves $50 per week at an 8 percent compounded interest rate will accumulate $756,385 by the age of 65. By contrast, a 35-year-old who saves the same amount at the same interest rate will have only $322,911 to show for her efforts—less than half as much. The sooner you start to save for retirement, the easier the task is.

2. Contribute the maximum you are allowed to any tax-favored savings plan available to you

This is what they call a no-brainer. If someone offers you $500, you take it, right? So why should it be different if that someone is the federal government? If you can shield your retirement income from taxes, that's the same as the federal government sending you a check. Accept it.

If your company has a 401 (k) program, or something similar, it's almost criminal not to make the maximum allowed tax-deductible contribution. That's because your contribution will usually trigger a contribution from your employer, who may pay anywhere from 25 cents to a dollar for every dollar you put in. And it will also be exempt from taxes—which means Uncle Sam is chipping in too. In addition, earnings in the account will accumulate tax-free.

The same goes for a Roth IRA. You qualify for one of these if you are single and have an adjusted gross income of less than $95,000, or if you are married and have an income of less than $150,000. Each working spouse can contribute $2,000 a year. Do it.

Unlike traditional IRAs, Roth IRAs don't give you an up-front tax deduction. But they do allow your savings to accumulate tax-free, and unlike other retirement savings plans, *they allow you to withdraw those earnings tax-free at retirement.* In most cases, that makes the Roth IRA more attractive than the traditional IRA, which gives you a tax-deduction up front, but requires you to pay taxes when you withdraw the money.

If you are self-employed, or earn some income on the side, set up a SEP-IRA. You'll be able to invest 13 percent of your self-employed earnings, deduct that amount from taxes, and allow earnings to accumulate tax-free—just like contributions to a 401 (k) or a traditional IRA.

The tricky question is whether to make *after-tax* contributions to a 401 (k) plan, which you can sometimes do after you've reached the maximum on your tax-deductible contributions, or make similar nondeductible contributions to a traditional IRA, which you can do if your income is too high for a Roth IRA.

These investments still allow your earnings to accumulate tax-free, but the earnings are taxable as ordinary income when you withdraw them. That's worth doing if you are going to invest in government securities or corporate bonds. But it may not be worth doing if you are going to invest in stocks or stock mutual funds. The capital gains on stocks aren't taxed until a stock is sold, and then they are taxed at the lower capital gains rate. So the tax advantages of just investing in stocks can often be better than those of making nondeductible contributions to your 401 (k) and IRA.

Another warning: It's probably not a good idea to mix deductible IRA contributions and nondeductible contributions in the same account. It can create a bookkeeping nightmare when retirement comes, since you'll have to pay taxes on the deductible contribution but not the nondeductible contribution.

And then there are variable annuities. These can be a much better buy than they used to be, if you shop around; competition has driven down the fees. But look carefully at the tax consequences. Annuity salespeople push them as a tax shelter. But putting money in annuities is like making nondeductible contributions to a 401(k) or traditional IRA. The earnings accumulate tax-free, but you'll have to pay ordinary income tax when you withdraw the money. If you are investing in bonds, or if you are going to hold on to your investment for a long time, that could be a good deal. If not, you may be better off just investing in stocks in a taxable account.

3. Once you've reached the maximum on every tax-favored savings account that's available to you, figure out how much more you need to save

The retirement savings calculator at SmartMoney.com can be a big help on this score. Use it first to calculate how much income you'll need at retirement—as a rule of thumb, assume you'll need 80 percent of your pre-retirement income.

Then fill in when you plan to retire and how long you think you and your spouse will live. (Be generous here, to make sure you don't run out of money before you die.) Add in how much money you've saved, and how much of a return—6, 7, 8 percent—you think you can earn on your savings. (Be conservative here, since there's little reason to think the stock market will provide the same returns in the next decade that it has in the past decade.)

Fill in your expected social security income; the government sends you an estimate each year, but if you don't have it handy, SmartMoney.com will do an estimate. Then let the calculator give you the results, telling you how much you need to save each year between now and the time you retire.

If you're lucky, the calculator will tell you that you're already doing enough to meet your retirement goals. More likely, it will give you a number that makes your eyes go buggy. Then it's time to move to Step 4.

4. Consider the new, fourth leg of the retirement stool: a job

Truth is, for most Americans, there's no real reason to stop working at 65 or 67. When Otto Von Bismarck created the first public pension system in Germany in 1891, the age for collecting benefits was set at 65, but the average life expectancy was just 45. Medical science has made it possible for us to live longer; it's also made it possible for us to work longer.

The social security rules have also been changed, to reduce the penalty on those who continue to work. Private pension plans, as mentioned above, are no longer designed to force people out at 65. And mandatory retirement has by and large been outlawed.

As a result, the long trend toward ever-earlier retirement has, in the last decade, begun to reverse itself.

My mother is an example. She continued to work full-time as a guidance counselor in the Chattanooga city schools. She doesn't volunteer her age to anyone, nor will I; and none of her coworkers dare ask. She works because she enjoys it, because she can use the money, and because she's still good at what she does.

Others have taken what are called bridge jobs to ease the transition between full-time work and complete retirement. These tend to be either part-time jobs or self-employment. A recent study on the subject by the Employee Benefit Research Institute said "estimates suggest that between one-third and one-half of older Americans will work on a bridge job before retiring completely."

5. Consider long-term-care insurance

As Americans live longer, they also increase the odds they'll end life in a nursing home as a result of Alzheimer's, a stroke, or some other debilitating illness of old age.

The price tag for long-term care is steep: Nursing homes cost an average of $40,000 per year—in some parts of the country, the tab runs to $100,000—and the price is expected to climb to five times that amount within thirty years. Home health aides charge as much as $36,000 per year, and that cost is expected to rise sharply as well.

Most older Americans rely on Medicare to pay their medical costs, but that program only pays for hospital stays and short-term, skilled nursing home stays after hospitalization. Medicaid, which was established in the 1960s to help low-income people with acute-care expenses, has become the single largest underwriter of long-term care. The program pays out $25.5 billion annually—more than half of its total outlays—for such care. But in order to qualify for Medicaid, you must first impoverish yourself. Besides a home, a car, and a burial plot, you're allowed an average of just $2,000 in liquid assets, depending on which state you live in. In order to qualify, many senior citizens feverishly spend down their assets before going into a nursing home.

Long-term-care insurance may provide the answer to that quandary. If you retire with less than $100,000 in assets, it's probably just as well to skip it, and let Medicaid pay the bill. If you retire with more than $1 million, you can afford to handle nursing home bills on your own—just set aside $160,000 as a contingency to pay for four years of long-term care. Only 10 percent of senior citizens who enter a nursing home stay more than four years; the average is two and a half years.

But if your assets at retirement are between $100,000 and $1 million, read on. You may want to take a close look at long-term-care insurance.

Long-term-care insurance debuted in the early 1970s. Back then, the typical policy covered nursing home stays, but not home care. Insurers reserved the right to unilaterally cancel policies. In the 1980s, coverage on many policies was expanded to include home care and expenses associated with Alzheimer's disease and dementia. By the 1990s, most policies paid for care in assisted-living facilities, had guaranteed-renewal clauses, and paid benefits for anywhere from two years to a lifetime's worth of long-term-care costs. Since 1990, half a million long-term-care policies have been sold annually. Some employers have begun offering long-term-care insurance as part of their standard benefits package.

Most people who buy policies do so to protect assets that they want to leave to their heirs—or to try to avoid becoming a financial burden to their families at the end of their lives.

When should you buy? There's a catch-22 here, since the cost of the policy rises sharply with your age. Most people can't afford to buy when they finally want to and don't want to buy when they can afford to.

I'd recommend waiting until you are in the 55- to 65-year-old range to consider purchasing long-term-care insurance. The policies are cheaper when you are younger, but they are in such a state of flux that you may end up with Model T coverage at a time when the Concorde is the standard. On the other hand, if you wait until your seventies, the policies can get prohibitively expensive, and you may develop signs of a disease—Alzheimer's, for instance—that will lead insurers to refuse coverage.

If you decide to shop for long-term-care insurance, take your time. It's incredibly complicated. And don't take your information from the insurance agent; most aren't that well informed and are too eager to sell. *Consumer Reports* periodically rates policies; get hold of their latest. Look for policies that cover all types of care at nursing homes, assisted-living facilities, and your own home. Unless you expect to need long-term care within the next few years, inflation protection and nonforfeiture clauses—which will boost your premium—are essential. The maximum inflation protection rate offered is 5 percent, about half of the annual increases in long-term care costs between 1985 and 1995, but better than nothing. Nonforfeiture clauses guarantee that the premiums you've paid will be applied to your long-term care costs if you allow your policy to lapse.

And bring your kids in on the decision. Truth is, you don't buy long-term care insurance for your health; Medicaid takes care of that, and most nursing homes accept Medicaid patients. You buy long-term care insurance to protect your assets, and your children are the ones who ultimately benefit from that.

12

Privacy in the New Economy

Your Life Is an Open Book

Michael Saylor wants to know everything about you. Not just your hobbies, likes and dislikes, or what kind of car you drive. Saylor wants you to tell him your entire medical history, every last detail about your finances, and everything you can think of about you and your family.

"I want to have your personality on file," the software entrepreneur says. "I need to have your *paranoias* on file."

Saylor's vision is to create the next generation of information business, which will be proactive—even telepathic—rather than reactive. His computers would know what you want, what you hate, what you need, what you fear. And they'd use that information to advise, inform, guide, and direct you. Twenty-four hours a day, seven days a week, via cell phone, pager, computer, or PalmPilot.

Saylor's futuristic vision is the logical next step in the technologically driven, service-oriented New Economy, and it has already made him a multibillionaire. His company, MicroStrategy, went public in June of 1998, giving him a net worth in March 2000 that exceeded ten billion dollars.

But to others, Saylor's dream sounds like a nightmare. A March 1998 *Business Week*/Harris poll showed that almost two-thirds of the many people who don't use the Internet are staying away because they are wary of losing their privacy. To some of those people, Saylor's notion of a computer network that tracks your every movement and knows your every fear has eerie echoes of George Orwell's classic book *1984:*

> There was of course no way of knowing whether you were being watched at any given moment. . . . You had to live, did live, from habit that became instinct—in the assumption that every sound you made was overheard, and, except in darkness, every movement scrutinized.

The differences between Orwell's nightmare and Saylor's dream, of course, are huge. Orwell envisioned a world in which the state used its all-knowing technological prowess to crush human emotion and desire. Saylor sees a world in which that technology works for you, to calm your fears and satisfy your desires.

Enter your stock portfolio into Saylor's Telepath program, and you'll be called, beeped, or e-mailed with news whenever a sudden market change threatens to affect you. If your child gets sick at school or a traffic tie-up threatens your commute home, you'll get word wherever you are. If tickets go on sale for a concert by one of your favorite bands, the computer will reserve four in your name and give you the opportunity to accept or reject them.

A fire in your neighborhood? Saylor's service will call you at work. A monster tornado ripping its way across your county at two o'clock in the morning? You'll get a call telling you to head for the cellar. Afraid your business partner is draining the company bank accounts and sending the money to the Cayman Islands for safe-keeping? MicroStrategy will give you a heads-up if there's any unusual account activity.

Saylor envisions a proactive intelligence network that will eventually become so ubiquitous, so universal—and so trusted—that you won't be able to imagine life without it, any more than you can imagine life without a telephone or electricity. "We want to be the General Electric of this business," says Saylor.

But still, for many, there's that nagging fear. Do I really want the computer to know *everything* about me? Do I want to live in a world where someone is keeping track of every book I buy, every medicine I use, every website I visit? In the New Economy, do I have any privacy left?

Answering that question may be one of the most difficult challenges facing the New Economy in the decade ahead. In the last two years, privacy has exploded as an issue in the U.S. Congress, with legislators on both sides of the aisle offering measures to restrict the flow of personal information. Conservative Republican Joe Barton of Texas made an unusual alliance with liberal Democrat Ed Markey of Massachusetts to sponsor amendments to a banking bill and an electricity deregulation bill on information privacy.

Yet heavy-handed legislation at this point could stunt the rapid growth and development of Internet-based businesses. In a world where information is the currency of exchange and customers are the greatest asset, *information about customers* is gold. In the old economy, Procter & Gamble made a product and then conducted a nationwide mass marketing campaign to convince you to buy it. In the New Economy, companies want information about you so they can anticipate your needs and wishes, and market products to you based on their knowledge of your desires.

Amazon.com is at the front end of this trend. The company monitors your purchases, and it puts a little piece of information in your computer's hard drive—known as a "cookie"—so it can identify you each time you visit its website. It then greets you by name and offers new book and record suggestions based on your past purchases.

That's just the beginning. As companies gain more experience monitoring your activity on the Internet, and sharing the information they gather, they will be better able to anticipate your every need. They will also learn to discriminate. If you're a proven discount shopper, you'll find you are constantly facing pitches to buy products at the lowest possible price. If you tend to go for higher-priced "prestige" products and services, then those will be marketed to you. The experience you have as you browse through computer sites will be unique; the advertisements you see, the products that are offered to you, the information available to you will all be customized, based on the huge store of information that's been accumulated about your preferences and habits.

In many cases, that will be a welcome, and timesaving, service. When you log on to your favorite newspaper, you'll immediately get news on the topics you care about most. When you go to your favorite clothes store, you'll immediately see the style of clothes you prefer to wear.

But the use of your personal information will also be, at times, annoying. If you buy a bag of pistachios online on a whim, you have to wonder how many e-mails pushing nuts you'll get in the weeks ahead. If you are pegged as a buyer of luxury rather than discount goods, you may never be shown the best prices.

And more than annoying, it could become dangerous. Consider the case of Ronald Thiemann, who was forced to step down from his post as head of Harvard Divinity School because he used his computer to visit pornographic sites. Or Bronte Kelly, who could not get work as a retail store clerk for several years because a database incorrectly listed him as a shoplifter.

Mining the Data

What makes all this possible are remarkable advances in what's known as *data mining*. Computer databases have been accumulating vast stores of information for decades. But the information has been of limited use, because it was so difficult to get at. In the last five years, however, the ability to quickly search vast stores of data and pull out relevant information has increased tremendously. As a result, information that has long been available to anyone willing to spend hours or days tracking it down is now instantly available.

Nora Paul is an expert in computerized information at the Poynter Institute for journalism. I called her one day and challenged her to see what she could find out about me, knowing nothing more than my name and the fact that I worked for *The Wall Street Journal* in Washington.

In little more than ten minutes, Paul had assembled a dossier. She knew my birth date, my social security number, my address, my weight, and where I had grown up. She also knew the same details for my wife. She knew what we had paid for our house in 1990, the names of all our neighbors, the names of our children's babysitters, and the makes of our cars. And she congratulated me for not receiving any recent traffic citations!

All of this information was gathered from government records that have long been open to the public. But they have never been as *accessible* to the public as they are today. For just $39, a company called U.S. Search (USSearch.com) will do a "super search" on anyone you ask, looking for addresses, phone numbers, neighbors, spouses, professional licenses, property ownership and value, vehicle ownership and value, and civil judgments. Try it on yourself; the information about you that is readily available, and just a few keystrokes away, will surprise you.

On top of that, huge stores of information are being accumulated about the purchases you make. If you use a credit card at the grocery store, for instance, the computer may be keeping a personalized list of everything you buy. And there's no question the computers at Amazon.com are doing the same.

Internet executives make a distinction between information that is very private and needs to be held in the strictest confidence—your credit card number, your finances, your medical records—and information that is, as Brett Bullington of Internet company Excite@Home puts it, "implied learning about someone, based on their preferences." He argues the industry has moved quickly to protect the first kind of information. "The momentum in this industry is to get behind this problem, because if we don't, consumers won't use our services," he says.

And to an extent, he's right. Most Internet shopping sites, for instance, use encryption to protect credit card purchases. As a result, using your credit card to buy something on the Internet is less dangerous than giving your credit card to a waitress in a restaurant.

In addition, many sites have moved in the last year or so to post explicit privacy policies. They tell you whether or not they sell information on you to other companies, and sometimes they give you an opportunity to opt out of personalized services, such as receiving direct e-mail solicitations.

"We know if we aren't honest with people who use the Internet, they are going to distrust this new service we are all putting out," Bullington says.

To be sure, the potential advantages of this next wave of personalized technology are immense. Have you ever booked a plane ticket, sat in traffic on the way to the airport, and waited twenty minutes to check in, only to discover that not only was your flight cancelled, but that you missed the only other flight that would get you there in time? MicroStrategy would sell you an I-ticket—the "I" stands for "intelligent"—which would monitor your itinerary, call you if anything changes, and rebook you on the next flight. It would even call the people you're meeting to tell them about the changes.

If you give your entire medical history to MicroStrategy's Provantage system, it promises to let you know if you buy a drug that your body won't like. If your doctor gets sued for malpractice, you'll know right away. After all, says Saylor, what matters more: your health or abstract concerns about privacy?

Over time, Saylor says, companies like MicroStrategy will have to earn your trust by promising complete confidentiality. "The most powerful asset in the world of the future is a trusted network," he says. Customers will flock to those they believe they can trust and steer clear of those which are deemed untrustworthy. In the end, giving information to a company like MicroStrategy, Saylor hopes, will be no different from giving your money to a bank. If you have trust in the company, you'll do it.

Privacy advocates counter that people trust banks because of a system of legal guarantees, enshrined in the Federal Reserve System, the Comptroller of the Currency's office, and the Federal Deposit Insurance Corporation (FDIC). Jason Catlett, president of Junkbusters.com, an Internet privacy group, says similar government actions may be needed to protect the consumer's online privacy. And Ari Schwartz, a policy analyst for the Center for Democracy and Technology, worries that the creation of a central repository of information will make it easier for the government to get its hands on that information or for the information to be subpoenaed in divorce or criminal proceedings.

Such questions ensure that privacy will become increasingly a matter for public debate in the years ahead. It's one of the issues that leads America Online's Steve Case to say that "over the next few years, the future of the Internet will be determined more by policy choices than technology choices."

Protecting Your Privacy

In the meantime, what can you do to protect your own privacy?

The first thing to do is take a deep breath and relax. Technology may be creating challenges to your privacy, but it's also creating solutions to those challenges. At the end of the day, the New Economy puts a great deal of control over privacy into your hands.

So the first question you have to answer is, Just how much privacy do you want?

Credit card purchases are a good example. Thanks to advanced encryption technology, credit card purchases made on the Internet are probably safer than purchases made over the telephone, or even in public restaurants and stores. After all, there's always the danger that a waitress or clerk may copy down your number or that someone nearby may grab a copy of the paper credit card slip.

Still, you can help ensure online credit card transactions are safe by giving out your number sparingly, and only on a secure web server. You can tell if you are on a secure server by the locked padlock that shows up on your web browser tool bar, if you are using Netscape Navigator, or at the bottom of the screen on Microsoft's Internet Explorer. You can also tell if the familiar "http" in the address line turns into "https"—the "s" meaning "secure." When you are on a secure server, your transaction is encrypted (put into code) by technology developed by computer experts at MIT. This makes it difficult, if not impossible, for even the most skilled hacker to make sense of the data.

Is there still a slight chance that a hacker can find your card number or, more likely, that an unscrupulous merchant will misuse the number? Yes, there's still a chance. But remember your credit card usually protects you after the first $50 of liability.

And if that's not enough protection to suit your taste, try the service available at Cybercash.com. Cybercash uses an even higher level of encryption technology to protect your credit card number and allows you to deal directly with a long list of merchants who accept Cybercash. The service can also let you take money directly out of your bank account for purchases.

E-mail is another area of concern for many computer users in the New Economy. E-mail messages can easily be tracked back to their sender, and e-mail addresses are readily available on the Internet. The result is increasing amounts of unwanted e-mail and junk e-mail, known colloquially as "spam." Moreover, e-mail messages often leave permanent records on the computer hard disk—witness the increasing tendency to subpoena computer hard disks in legal cases. At *The Wall Street Journal,* our lawyers warn us to assume anything we write in an e-mail message may show up one day in court.

But technology is already providing a solution to this problem, for those who need it. Free online services like Anonymizers.com and Ziplip.com enable you to send anonymous e-mail messages. Anonymizers remails your message from a server that can't be traced, although remailing can take a day or two. Ziplip posts your message on a website, then sends an e-mail message to the recipient telling him or her to come retrieve it.

Lucent Technologies offers an even more sophisticated technological answer: target-revocable e-mail. Under this system, each e-mail you send goes out, in effect, with a different return address, although all return addresses lead back to you. If any of your e-mails result in unwanted responses, you can simply revoke those particular addresses without disturbing other incoming messages.

And what to do about those secret little "cookies" that some websites insert in your hard drive, so they can track your activity? Well, most browsers will allow you to set your Preferences feature so that the browser either won't accept cookies or will alert you each time a cookie comes your way. If you are using a Netscape 4 browser, for instance, you can click on the Edit menu, then choose Preferences, then look under Advanced. The browser will give you options for dealing with cookies. On the Internet Explorer 4.0 browser, use the View menu, click Internet Options and then Advanced, and look at the settings under Security.

The problem here is that those little cookies can often be extremely useful; they allow you to avoid registering the second time you visit a site, for instance, or they allow Amazon.com to alert you to custom book offerings or to know your billing and shipping information without prompting.

A more sophisticated solution may be to buy the well-reviewed Cookie Pal software, available from Kookaburra Software at kburra.com. This software can be set up to automatically reject certain cookies, while letting others in, according to your specifications. It will also keep a summary of cookies that have been accepted and those that have been rejected. It costs $15.

Complete privacy freaks might want to buy Anonymizer's (anonymizer.com) Window Washer software. It costs $29.95 and will completely clean out your computer's cache of cookies, as well as its history of the websites you've visited.

Help for Cyber-Parents

If you're like most of us, your children will quickly surpass you in their skills navigating the Internet. But that can create problems. Pornography is rampant on the Internet. Pedophiles cruise children's chat rooms, trying to strike up relationships. And scam operators will try to convince your kids to provide them information about you and your family that they can sell.

For help in dealing with the challenge, take a look at netparents.org. The site provides some useful tips on computer use for families. For instance, it suggests you place the computer in the family room or an open area of your home, that you take time to cruise the Internet with your children, and that you teach them to never give out personal information and never plan face-to-face meetings alone with online acquaintances.

Technology can help here too. At NetNanny.com, you can buy filtering software that will provide a list of sites your children can go to, and a list they can't go to—with regular updates of the lists that you can download for free. In addition, you can develop your own screening list for certain prohibited sites, words, and subjects. The cost is only $26.95.

And you can take some comfort from the fact that the government has gotten on the case of online merchants who collect information from kids. In August 1998, a popular website called GeoCities was forced to settle charges brought by the Federal Trade Commission that it used children's contests to collect personal information on children and their families, which it then shared with others. Since then, the FTC has also issued a notice of intention to issue rules governing the collection of information from and about children. Among other things, the FTC wants websites to obtain consent from parents before taking information from children. For more information, try the FTC's consumer-friendly website, at Ftc.com.

Ten Tips for Protecting Your Privacy in the New Economy

Remember, the power is in your hands. But you've got to use it. You can do more than anyone else to protect your own privacy. For starters, we recommend the following ten steps. For additional tips, try Junkbusters.com.

1. Never give your credit card number to anyone who calls you

They may not be who they say they are. If you are determined to accept a telemarketing offer, tell them you'll call back. That gives you a chance to check them out, first.

2. If you get an unwanted telemarketing phone call, don't hang up

Instead, insist that they put you on their "don't call" list. Telemarketers are required to maintain such lists and to refrain from calling the people on them for five years. If they don't, you may be able to sue for up to $1,500.

3. If you'd prefer not to get any telemarketing calls, write to the Direct Marketing Association

Ask to be put on their national "no-call" list. The address is P.O. Box 9014, Farmingdale, NY 11735-9014. Keep in mind that this association is funded by the people who are making all those annoying calls in the first place, so they may not have your interests at heart. On the other hand, if you make it clear you aren't going to purchase anything over the telephone, it's a waste of their time to call you anyway.

4. Ignore "product registration" cards

Usually, these are just an attempt to get more information out of you. With major purchases, simply save your receipts and the product warranty information, and you'll have the same protection.

5. Treat your e-mail messages as if they were postcards

There's not much difference, in terms of the privacy they afford you. Look for another way to communicate truly private messages. Also, avoid giving out your e-mail address as much as possible.

6. Look for a clear privacy statement before giving information on any website

If there isn't a privacy statement, move on. If there is, read it closely. It should tell whether the website plans to sell the information it collects from you. The statement may also give you an opportunity to opt out of having your information sold or of having it used in other ways.

7. Write the three largest credit bureaus, and ask them to stop selling your name

Also request the latest copy of your credit report, so you can see if there are any mistakes. The three big ones are Trans Union, Equifax, and Experian. You can call one toll-free number (1-888-567-8688) to ask that all three take you out of any information they sell to mailing lists. And you can request your own credit report online, at transunion.com, equifax.com, and experian.com.

8. Try to avoid giving out your social security number

If your state's division of motor vehicles uses the social security number on your driver's license, ask if they'll assign you a random driver's license number instead.

9. Don't let salesclerks write your credit card or social security number on your checks

That's just one more unnecessary way in which your number can get ripped off.

10. Check out online businesses before handing over money

There's probably some advantage to dealing with companies you've heard of. If you haven't heard of them, try checking them out on Bizrate.com, which uses the customers of online firms to rate them. Keep in mind that online merchants participate in Bizrate by choice; if they aren't listed, it could mean they have a problem.

Conclusion

The Power Is Yours—Now Use It!

It is difficult to live in the United States at the turn of the millennium and not be optimistic about the future.

The constant threat of annihilation that was part of the Cold War world has been eliminated. The once-confident predictions of American economic decline have been thoroughly disproven. And two centuries of dismal predictions about the dehumanizing effects of technology—from Mary Shelley's *Frankenstein* to *Fahrenheit 451*—have been discredited.

Instead, the century that witnessed history's great struggle with communism and fascism has ended in a remarkable celebration of human freedom. The walls that separate nations have crumbled, and national borders have become increasingly permeable to the flow of people, products, capital, and information. Technology has not devalued the individual human life; it has elevated it, creating new opportunities, new connections, new freedoms. The human imagination has not been suppressed; it has been liberated, in ways unimaginable even a decade or two ago. To be alive in America today is to face an exhilarating array of choices. For ever more people, life is not a burden they must bear, but an opportunity they can use to mold and fashion an existence that suits their interests and their skills.

Those of us who enjoy this wealth of choices need to remember that we are still a distinct minority. Most of the earth's population continues to live from day to day, with few choices and little power to do anything more than struggle for survival. And it's far from clear that the New Economy will make their plight better.

I participated in a day-long conference recently on the future of the Internet, jointly sponsored by Dow Jones & Co. Inc. and the Harvard Business School. At first, it focused on narrow, business-related questions—the future of e-commerce. But as the day wore on, the topic became more expansive, and the participants began to discuss the issue of how far the benefits of this economic revolution will spread.

The group divided, roughly, into two camps. On one side were the optimists, convinced the Internet would spur a great populist revolution that would spread its blessings around the globe. It would melt divisions of geography and nationality, allowing any-one, anywhere, to log on and partake of the great global feast of in-formation and commerce. The Internet might be a toy of the elite at the moment; but it would become the salvation of poor nations and poor people in the decades to come.

On the other side were the realists, pointing out that the last three decades have seen a disturbing widening of the gap between rich and poor people, and rich and poor nations. The economics of the New Economy—which often drive companies to grow ever-larger in order to take advantage of network economies or to capi-talize on well-known brand names—may make that gap even wider in the future.

The mythology of the New Economy is built around the romantic notion of high-school dropouts puttering in their parents' garages and building a gizmo that turns them into billionaires. But the reality of the New Economy may be something more like Microsoft, a behemoth of a company that either gobbles up or tears down its competitors. In a winner-take-all world, the losers have less to look forward to.

Moreover, even for those of us who enjoy its many benefits, the New Economy has its dark side. The opportunities are greater, but so are the risks. Individuals have more freedom to fashion their own existence, but also more responsibility to deal with the consequences if their efforts fail.

While the techno-romanticists talk hopefully about the creation of virtual communities, there are signs aplenty that the new world is creating more alienation and more antisocial behavior as well. David Thorburn, in an essay in *The American Prospect* magazine, writes:

> The computer encourages joining, interaction, sharing, the creation of communities of interest. Yet it is also congenial to our uncivic preferences for isolation, the avoidance of human contact, solipsism, lurking, voyeurism. Through its power to confer anonymity, it feeds instincts for scandal, revenge, name-calling, surveillance, pornography.

In the future, the challenges technology poses for human dignity seem certain to grow. The electronic technology revolution has been reasonably benign; the coming biotechnology revolution may be less so. It's now clear we will soon have the ability to predict the

characteristics of children before they are born and to alter funda-
mental aspects of human nature. That will open up a whole new
universe of choices. Who will dare to make them?

In the future, electronic and biological sciences will combine in
new and unthinkable ways. We already have pacemakers that help
keep human hearts on track; why not brain chips that enable people
to keep the entire contents of the Encylopedia Britannica stored in
their head? Once the right "interfaces" are developed, the world of
biological intelligence and electronic intelligence will connect, creating possibilities that make Mary Shelley's fantasy seem timid. In
the face of such extreme choices, how will we retain the essence of
our humanity?

If the history of the last two decades has taught us anything, it
should be that forecasting such things is a tricky business. No one a
generation ago came close to imagining the world we live in today;
so why should any of us presume we can forecast the world a generation from now?

That said, I choose to be an optimist. Human history doesn't
run in straight lines, but I do believe it progresses. Yes, there will be
panics; there will be reversals; there will be disasters. Poverty will
not be eliminated in a generation. Freedom will suffer setbacks.
There will be moments when humanity seems in danger of losing
its essence or when the world seems ready to descend into chaos.

But the lesson of the New Economy that characterizes American
society at the turn of the millennium is this: Human progress
means giving people more freedom, more choices, more power to
fashion their lives as they see fit. This book is designed to help in
that endeavor.

It's a great moment to be alive. Make the most of it.

ACKNOWLEDGMENTS

Like most books, this one is the result of a collaboration of many people.

First and foremost, credit goes to Keith Perine, who researched and drafted significant portions of the book. His keen mind and skilled research abilities made this book possible. He clearly has a great future ahead of him in journalism.

In addition, I'd partularly like to thank *The Wall Street Journal* for making it possible for me to do this book. Special thanks to Peter Kann, the chief executive, and Paul Steiger, the managing editor; also to Dan Hertzberg, Steve Adler, Jim Pensiero, Barney Calame, John Brecher, and Cathy Panagoulias. Without their support and forbearance, this book wouldn't have happened. Thanks also to Al Hunt, who brought me to *The Wall Street Journal* and encouraged and supported me once I arrived.

Many *Journal* colleagues enriched this book in various ways. David Wessel deserves special mention; he helped shape the proposal and made useful suggestions throughout the process; Chapter 8, in particular, was his idea. I couldn't have done the book without the support of Jerry Seib, who filled in for me when I was preoccupied. Greg Ip was particularly helpful in shaping Chapter 7, and Tom Petzinger provided useful comments as well. Works by Jake Schlesinger, George Anders, Walter Mossberg, Jonathan Clements, and Kara Swisher all contributed. Thanks also to Steve Schwartz, who does a wonderful job at *Smart Money.* And special thanks to the entire Washington bureau of the *Journal;* they're the best in the business. Thanks also to Mitchell Patterson for helping to check the final manuscript.

What's great about writing a book on the New Economy is that *everyone* is a part of it. That has given me an opportunity to draw on the expertise of many long-time friends: Bruce Gellin and Nancy Chockley on health care; Ted Bracken on educational financing; Rob Rosiello on Internet business models; Tom Darden on venture capital; Larry Summers on all things economic. Thanks also to Ron Fletcher and Clarence Kettler, who carried a draft of this book on their boat trip and provided useful comments. And to Mona Hanford, who is a brand of her own.

I've made many new friends in the course of this book, as well. Russ Ramsey and his colleagues at Freidman, Billings and Ramsey were extremely generous and helpful on the venture capital chapter. Raul Fernandez at Proxicom was helpful on all things regarding the Internet, and his colleague Scott McDonald was particularly helpful on electricity deregulation. David Gardner at the Motley Fool was also a great help.

I've drawn on the work of many other authors, among them John Schwartz of *The Washington Post,* and Paul Starobin of the *National Journal.* An article by Bradford De Long and Michael

Froomkin was particularly helpful. And many books have helped enlighten me, including Carl Shapiro and Hal Varian's *Information Rules,* Kevin Kelly's *New Rules for the New Economy,* Michael Wolf's *The Entertainment Economy,* Todd Buchholz's *Market Shock,* Lester Thurow's *Building Wealth,* and, of course, Bob Davis and David Wessel's *Prosperity.*

I owe a special debt to Neal Freeman, who first helped me understand the value of combining big-picture economic analysis with practical advice. Also to Peter Osnos, who first got me into the book business, and Peter Bernstein, who saw value in this book idea and pushed me to do it.

My agent in this and all things is Bob Barnett, who also encouraged me to do the project. My editor was John Mahaney, who has been a useful compatriot and sounding board throughout the project and who pushed me to make this a better book than I thought it could be. Thanks also to his assistant, Luke Mitchell.

And finally, thanks to my family—Lori, Lucyann, and Amanda—who tolerated me through all of this. In particular, the month we spent at the beach, with me writing, Lori reading and advising on my drafts, and the children playing, turned out to be far more rewarding than any of us could have imagined.

Index

255